Supernatural MOTHERING

WHERE GOD'S PRESENCE & POWER INVADE MOTHERHOOD

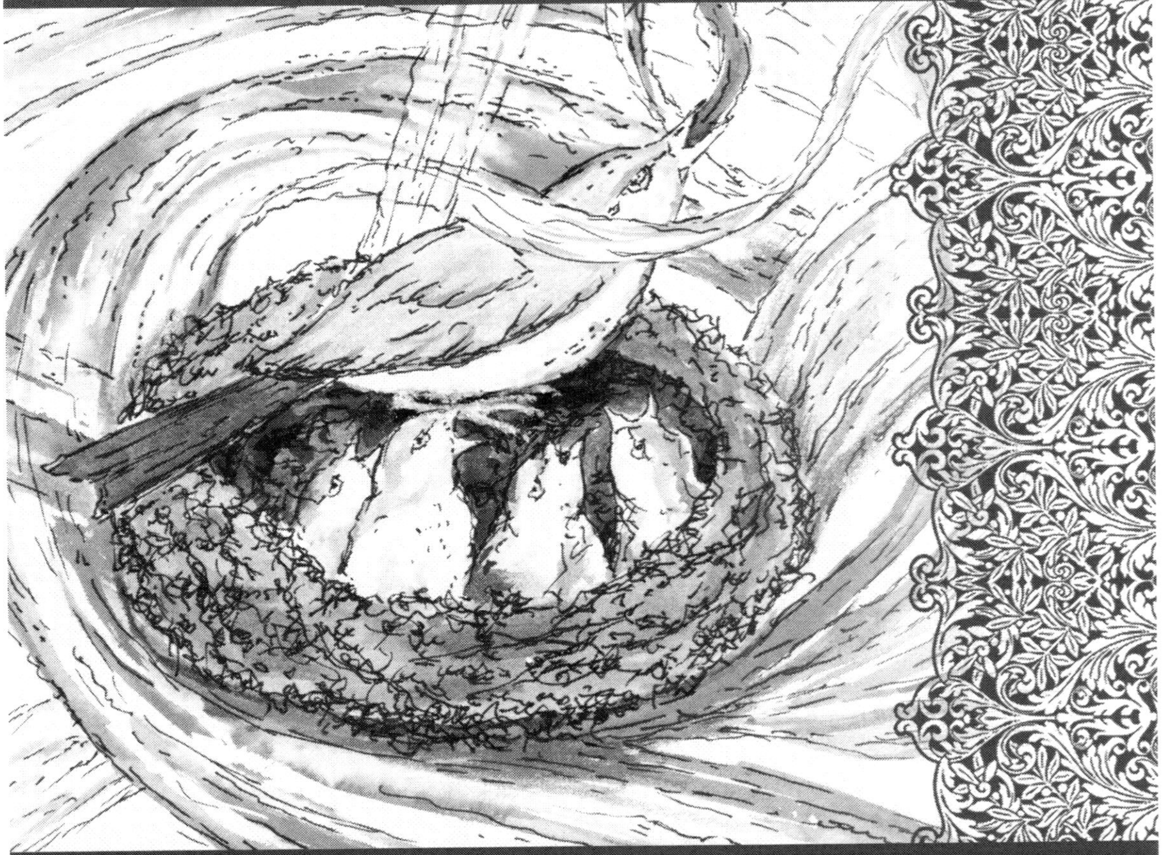

BOOK ONE

ASHLEY BRENDLE

www.SupernaturalMothering.org

This workbook has been designed
to be used as a personal study or within a group study

Cover & Interior Design and Interior Formatting — Lorraine Box (PropheticArt@sbcglobal.net)
Cover Art/Illustrator — Paul Farnham

ISBN-13: 978-1482341300
ISBN-10: 1482341301

Endorsements

Ashley's insight, practicality, transparency and vulnerability are refreshing and disarming! Your heart will be opened up to amazing Holy Spirit breathed revelation gleaned from the stories, biblical truths and activities this study provides. Do this as an individual, get some friends together or do it as a women's study at your church...but do it!

Your spirit will soar and you will be changed as you gain Heaven's perspective and the authority to operate in who God has called you to be as a world changing individual, wife and mother in these last days. Blessing, grace and anointing as you move through the pages of this study and experience the help, encouragement and shift He has for you!

— Lori Byrne, mother of four
Co-Founder, *Love After Marriage* Workshops, Bethel Church, Redding, California
Author, *Love After Marriage*

God wants to be involved with every aspect of our lives and has given us all we need to access His grace for every occasion, even difficult mothering moments. In *Supernatural Mothering,* Ashley has given us a great tool for the journey of finding God's heart for us as women who walk in His power and presence. Reading it and giving yourself to the activities will lead you deeper in your relationship with the Lord and change the way you parent. Ashley's life is living proof that God has strength, grace and wisdom for all who will call on Him.

— Janine Mason, mother of four
Co-Director, *Dream Culture*, Bethel Church, Redding, California
Author, *Dream Culture: Bringing Dreams to Life*

What I love about Ashley is that she genuinely practices what she preaches. Ashley is comfortable being a work-in-progress and sharing her victories as well as her struggles. She is also an overcomer in every way. This makes her material and overall ministry one that moms can deeply connect to. She has put together a powerful workbook. It's a proven fact that we change most when we engage material and work through what we learn.

This workbook is designed for just that purpose. It provides tools and exercises to help women move from defeat and negativity toward freedom and victory emotionally. In our society, we gravitate to quick fixes and instant breakthrough and yet this is not reality. Breakthrough happens incrementally as we purpose to align our thoughts and lives with God's truth. If a mom purposes to engage this material hope, breakthrough, and true joy in mothering will be some of the many benefits! I thoroughly endorse this workbook to moms who want to experience more of God in their homes!

— Olivia Shupe, mother of four
Founder & Director, *Raising Tomorrow's Leaders*, Bethel Church, Redding, California
Author, *Renaissance Kids*

Ashley Brendle has written a beautiful study that brings deep encouragement and Holy Spirit insight into our daily walk as mothers. She also places it in the perfect setting of being read and enjoyed in the context of fellowship with other mothers. I found it to be full of hope and joy and Heaven's perspective. I can almost hear the angels cheering me on as I disciple my precious children! It is so lovely and also so practical - like an abundant garden in your backyard - bringing beauty and nourishment for your family at the same time!

— Wendy Tang, mother of six
Co-leader, *Raising Tomorrow's Leaders,* Bethel Church, Redding, California

Believe me, you want to read this book if you desire to let God into your mothering wholeheartedly. It is an invitation to submit your mother's heart to God's and to discover He is extremely passionate about you and about your relationship with your children. Ashley shares out of her big, beautiful mother's heart, which is not only given to her for her own children, but to mother mothers as well.

— Teresa Slater, mother of two
M.A. in Counseling Psychology
Counselor, Transformation Center, Bethel Church, Redding, California
Counselor, Inner Healing, Mountain Chapel, Weaverville, California

I found Ashley's writing style warm and engaging. I could relate to her stories and found comfort in hearing similar struggles in motherhood. The studies are condensed but so powerful. They are very doable for a mother's schedule.

— Paris Lewis, mother of five
Heart of the Valley House of Prayer, Corvallis, Oregon

I've done many Bible studies, but in this study the Word became alive, connecting to my very DNA as a mother. I've been transformed as the study encouraged me to be real with my limitations and negative thinking. Ashley invites a Heavenly exchange through encounters with Holy Spirit, receiving Kingdom thinking, joy, and practical strategies to live out your true identity. Each weekly study has been life changing.

— Rose Roth, mother of two

This study is a surprising avenue of healing in the quiet times of a busy mom's life. I encourage mothers to carve out ten minutes a day to do the study. It will minister to their own hearts so that they can effectively minister to the hearts of their family.

— Erika Bond, mother of four

Thank you Ashley for this book, *Supernatural Mothering*. You yourself manifest grace, wisdom, ease and joy as you lovingly lead your seven happy children in supernatural mothering. This book is a treasure trove full of God given wisdom and inspiring help as you prayerfully, lovingly, and supernaturally guide your precious children in the ways of the Lord. Mothers and children and all will be greatly blessed as they apply the treasures imparted in this book.

Dear Mothers,

What an amazing and precious gift the Lord blesses us with, the gift of being a mother. In Psalm 127:3, the Lord says, "Lo, children are an heritage of the Lord: and the fruit of the womb is his reward." The book you hold in your hands, *Supernatural Mothering* is a gift to help mothers and grandmothers be a blessing to the "Gifter," our Lord God who has trusted us with oaks to raise as oaks of righteousness before Him (see Isaiah 61:9).

I am finding *Supernatural Mothering* very inspiring as I pray and spend time with our 24 wonderful grandchildren, who are teaching us to watch and pray more diligently as they grow and mature.

— Marge Lottis, mother of three, grandmother of 24

Dedication

I dedicate this book to my husband, Eric,

whose life has taught me so much about living by faith

and loving unconditionally.

His belief in me and his support help me soar!

And to my seven wonderful children,

who are the greatest of gifts

and the greatest of refiner's fire for this mama.

You are my best contribution to the world!

I love being your mama!

Small Group Invitation

We are created for community. Although this study is powerful even when done alone, its impact is taken to a whole new level in a small group setting. The ongoing give and take of support, ministry and fellowship you receive in the context of a small group is life-changing. We need each other. I am convinced it is "together with all the saints" where we tangibly experience the magnitude of God's love (Ephesians 3:18-19 HSBC)! Don't miss this opportunity to join with other mothers on this journey!

Join or lead a *Supernatural Mothering Small Group* in your church or community.

- Experience intimate friendships as you share the struggles and victories of motherhood with other trusted moms.
- Share and receive revelation and impartation of God's character and your true identity in a group setting.
- Enlarge your capacity to minister by actively participating in small group ministry time.

If you are interested in…

- **Joining a** *Supernatural Mothering Small Group*

Journey with other moms toward victorious, Christ-filled motherhood! Find a small group in your area at our website, **www.supernaturalmothering.org.** If there isn't one available, we'd love for you to join us online at **www.supernaturalmothering.org/online-bible-study.**

- **Leading a** *Supernatural Mothering Small Group*

Help lead this movement of mothers who are hungry for a deep connection to God's presence and power in motherhood! We highly encourage you to start a small group under your church's covering. Download an informational packet and letter to pastors/leaders at **www.supernaturalmothering.org/about-the-small-group-ministry.** Present it to your church leadership. Next, purchase the *Leader's Guide* through our webstore for everything you need to get started!

The Leader's Guide includes:

- meeting outlines
- discussion questions
- ministry tools
- handouts
- "Practicing His Presence" exercises and more!

Join the *Supernatural Mothering* network!

Register with us at **www.supernaturalmothering.org/leaders-register-your-group**. We'll pray for you, support you through our Facebook group just for registered leaders, and share your small group and church affiliation on our website for the benefit of other mothers seeking to join a group.

Contents

Introduction	1	
Study Components: An Overview	3	
Beauty For Ashes: My Spiritual Journey	9	
Your Competence Is From God	**13**	week one
The Power of Renewing Your Mind	**23**	week two
The Strategic Mother	**33**	week three
Walking in Christ's Authority	**43**	week four
Freedom from Generational Sin	**53**	week five
The Peaceful Mother	**63**	week six
Entering His Rest	**71**	week seven
Everything You Need	**81**	week eight
A Wise Woman Builds Her House	**95**	week nine
Releasing the Kingdom in Your Home	**109**	week ten
The Joyful Mother	**119**	week eleven
The Promised Outpouring	**129**	week twelve
Having Trouble Hearing God?	143	
Supernatural Mothering Ministries	147	
Acknowledgments	149	
Works Cited	151	
Blank Pages for Drawing	153	

Introduction

Motherhood is quite a journey! It can be all-consuming from diapers to diplomas as we intimately walk with these gifts, our children, from conception to adulthood. Many mothers feel isolated in their homes while trying to stay afloat amidst the rushing currents of motherhood. Yet we were not meant to take this journey alone.

The purpose of this study is to ignite a dialogue between you and Holy Spirit. It will equip you to walk in your true identity and authority as a mother. It isn't a book you just sit back and read. This study will challenge you. It will force you to ask hard questions; to even sit with them, perhaps unanswered, for a while.

You'll be encouraged to take steps of faith on the truth and revelation you already possess while seeking more. You'll need a willingness to be healed, to go deeper, and to let God uncover areas that may have been hidden. Not everyone is willing to go there. Not everyone is ready.

But I hope you will join me and a number of other mothers who are rising up with courage to take this journey. This study empowers you to link arms with Jesus and other mothers. With the power and presence of Holy Spirit, you will be changed.

As a result, you will be better equipped to pass on the Kindgom of God to the next generation! The outcome is strong families who bring Heaven to earth in their homes, communities and nation. You won't approach motherhood the same again. I'm so glad we're in this together!

Joy in the journey,

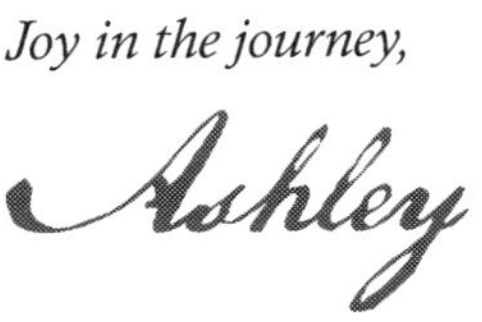

Study Components

AN OVERVIEW

This study is designed to be interactive with ample space for you to journal. However, there may be some who prefer to illustrate what God is showing them. Because God speaks in numerous ways, through words and pictures, I want to encourage you to capture what He is saying in ways that best communicate to your heart. Additional blank pages have been provided at the back of the workbook for those who like to draw or sketch.

THE KEY VERSE...

serves as an anchor of the truth you'll be securing throughout the week.

day one

THE STORY...

illustrates this truth with examples from my own journey and from the journey of others.

THE DAILY DECLARATION...

is to be said every day of the week's study. This is a blueprint for a new mindset and identity. The declarations are based on Scripture. God's word won't return void. It will accomplish what He intends in your life (Isaiah 55:11).

Declarations serve as a starting point in believing who the Bible says you are even if your life doesn't yet reflect it. This is the place where the power of agreement starts to shift things. You empower what you agree with.

In the Garden of Eden, Eve believed and agreed with the serpent's lie. Her belief in a lie led to sinful action and she ate the fruit from the tree of good and evil. In doing so, she gave Satan authority over her that previously was nonexistent. Thanks be to God, through the reality and power of the cross, we have been given back this authority!

Declarations help you believe and confess the reality of your salvation. You are saved, healed and delivered. It doesn't only matter what you believe. It is also crucial what you confess!

"If you confess with your mouth 'Jesus is Lord' and believe in your heart that God raised him from the dead, you will be saved. One believes with the heart, resulting in righteousness, and one confesses with the mouth, resulting in salvation."

Romans 10:9-10 HCSB

"From the words of his mouth a man will enjoy good things..."

Proverbs 13:2 HCSB

If you find the declaration is difficult to say and believe, it could be you have a stronghold or a lie in that area. The study is designed to help you tackle these lies through the ministry of Holy Spirit and God's Word. Don't give up! Dig deeper. The Lord wants to help you breakthrough to the other side!

I encourage you to post the week's declaration or carry it with you wherever you go. Keep it within reach. Continually renew your mind with it! Believe what it says about you and about God. The declarations have been written to propel you into a new realm of victorious motherhood!

IN A NUTSHELL...

is a bite-size summary you can easily tuck in your heart and mind. Memorize and repeat it to yourself when you confront old mindsets or want a fresh connection with God's truth.

day two

READ & REFLECT...

gives additional reinforcement of the powerful truth introduced to you on Day One. Your written reflections open up communication between you and God on the subject.

Your gut-level response to the truth in the Scripture and the questions that follow give you clues as to whether you really believe it or not. You will begin to uncover any lies or unbelief you may be holding against the truth.

If you've been in the church long enough, you've learned the "proper" response to various Scripture. I encourage you to be raw and real. Be honest so you can face and discern what your heart is really saying.

"You will know the truth, and the truth will set you free."

John 8:32 HCSB

Knowing the truth about the state of your own heart and the truth of God's promises will advance your breakthrough.

day three

HEART-TO-HEART WITH HOLY SPIRIT...

is designed to be a progressive dialogue between you and Holy Spirit. It's a customized journey He'll take you on and He will gently lead you. Through it, He'll bring you to new levels of healing, revelation and wholeness.

Some women will be accustomed to regularly hearing God's voice. While for others, it may take some time. Let me reassure you. You do hear Him. He's speaking all the time. Be patient. Don't rush. He will woo you closer with His love.

"The sheep that are my own hear and are listening to My voice; and I know them, and they follow me."

John 10:27 AMP

In addition, you may already have a well-developed prayer life. However, I have written prayers to assist you in your conversation with Holy Spirit. Feel free to use these and to personalize them further. They are intended to jump start you on your heart-to-heart journey with Jesus!

For this section, it is helpful to find someplace quiet (I know this isn't easy). You may want to play worship or soaking music to set the atmosphere. Burn a candle or go outside into nature and sit with your workbook. Do whatever you need to do to connect and get cozy with Jesus.

Be still. Listen. Believe you can hear His voice and He wants to speak to you. If you've joined a *Supernatural Mothering Small Group*, each meeting you will participate in short but sweet exercises practicing His presence and gaining greater confidence in hearing His voice.

For further information on the subject, please read *"Having Trouble Hearing God?"* on page 143.

day four

FAITH IN ACTION...

helps you further appropriate the healing and truth you've received on Day Three. It's an opportunity to personalize it for yourself. Your actions, even if small, will solidify God's work and propel you forward! They will integrate these truths into the fabric of your life.

"Show me your faith without works, and I will show you faith from my works....
You see that faith was active together with his works,
and by works, faith was perfected."

James 2:18, 22 HCSB

Let your faith be perfected even more as you act on it!

day five

STONES OF REMEMBRANCE JOURNAL...

You've done your part. You've been courageous enough to embark on the week's journey. You've confidently approached His throne. You've confronted lies and repented of any sin or unbelief. You've invited His presence and His input into intimate areas of your life. Now, you are believing and acting on His truth. Watch Him bear the fruit of this in you and around you!

Day Five is for observing God's faithful and powerful action on your behalf. Approach it with hopeful expectation! He is capable of "taking things from here." Of course, this doesn't mean you just coast. You and Jesus are a team!

The deep uprooting has been accomplished but you may need to again "take every thought captive" (2 Corinthians 10:4-5 HCSB). You can always return to Day Three and walk through the process again with Holy Spirit. By continually acknowledging and submitting to Him, you are intentionally maintaining the new ground God has gained in your life.

Let this day serve as an ongoing record or journal of God's help and intervention – a place to give testimony of His loving activity on your behalf.

AN OVERVIEW

"Then Samuel took a stone and set it between Mizpah and Shen,
and he called the name of it Ebenezer (stone of help) saying,
Heretofore the Lord has helped us."

I Samuel 7:12 AMP

This day marks the stones of remembrance set up along your personal journey. You can return to these and remember God's continual faithfulness to you in the past, present and future. Be sure to share God's activity in your life with your children as well.

Use the extra space provided to journal your responses and thoughts throughout the week. If you are taking part in a small group, this is a great place to record insights from the other moms along with the prophetic words you receive.

Beauty For Ashes

MY SPIRITUAL JOURNEY

Everyone has a unique story to tell. I am honored you would hear mine. Each person's story is intermingled with joy and sorrow. Ultimately, mine is a love story of being lost then found.

AND SO MINE BEGINS

My life always seems to begin and in some ways end at age three. It was at this age my dad left my mom and their marriage ended in divorce. My earliest memories are marked with a sense of abandonment, rejection and fear. I wasn't conscious of these lies that filtered my world well into adulthood. But I grew up in their soil. At age three, a little girl was lost. I had to grow up fast in order to cope with the many crises around me.

My mom raised my brother and me. She worked diligently to provide for our needs. Between her and my dad, I never lacked anything. In fact, I was quite spoiled. But all the riches in the world couldn't fill the hole inside of me. At the young age of six, in a Sunday school classroom, I chose to follow Jesus.

But it would be years before I felt like I knew Him face to face. In search of self-worth, I threw myself into my school work and an excessive amount of extra-curricular activities. I was your typical over-achiever. But no amount of accolades could prove to me I was precious and loved. The other messages spoke too loudly.

Appearance was highly valued in my family. I tried to fix things from the outside in, or at least fool everyone else with how I looked. I swayed from over-eating to anorexia in my early twenties. Others may have been convinced I had it all together, but the only person I could never totally deceive was myself.

MARRIAGE AND MISSIONS

I met and married my sweet husband Eric in 2001. Neither of us was aware of the extent of brokenness I had buried deep inside. It would expose itself occasionally. I had been to counseling, but I just couldn't shake it.

We went as missionaries to Corsica, France a month after our honeymoon. It had been my dream. I was crazy about anything and everything French. I had fallen in love with Eric who had a similar passion for this people and nation. We were quite a match.

But the intensity and estrangement of the mission field were too much for me. I had already been trying to cope with "normal" life armed with less than necessary. The mission field was a perfect catalyst for things to start coming to the surface. After three and a half years there, we left to furlough in England.

It was during this time, at a retreat center in Switzerland, I first came in touch with the root of much of my pain. I had been orphaned. Not literally. My parents did love me, that much I knew. But for various reasons, they had been absent during my childhood. The lack of my father's physical presence and his inability for intimacy had left me fatherless. My mom stayed by my side but had so much of her own pain to process, she wasn't emotionally available. I hadn't seen my life in this light before. To an extent, I had been forced to raise myself as an orphan.

THE SPIRIT OF ADOPTION

This began my journey of hungering for adoption. A few years later, we moved to Redding, California so Eric could be a student at the Bethel School of Supernatural Ministry. I spent about a year benefiting from their Sozo aftercare ministry. I allowed myself to deeply grieve and confront the losses of my childhood. I learned to forgive. I experienced deliverance from fear and other oppression. I tasted real freedom for the first time.

I remember thinking, *So, this is what it's like to live without constant anxiety.* It had been a deceptive companion all those years. Yet it was familiar. I began to live life from a different viewpoint. No longer as an orphan but as a found, chosen child in intimate relationship with the Father, Son and Holy Spirit. I had met my Heavenly Father and encountered His love for me. Life would never be the same!

A LIFE-CHANGING ENCOUNTER

One particular encounter became a significant crossroads for me. In my minds-eye, I saw a theatre with a stage and red cushioned seats. The theatre was completely empty. However, in the front row, there were two reserved seats, one marked for Dad and one for Mom. A cord was drawn in front of them forbidding anyone else from taking their places. Jesus stood in the aisle, waiting.

He wanted to know if I was willing to remove the reserved signs for them and let Him take their seats instead. I was afraid. For years, I had waited for these roles to be totally and sufficiently filled by my parents. But this often left me wanting. I had a choice to make.

Would I let Papa God and Holy Spirit become the father and mother I had always dreamed of? Would I let Papa God meet those deep needs from infancy into adulthood? Would I let Him mother me? Would I let Him father me?

Saying yes would mean I could release my parents to Him. The little girl locked inside would no longer need my earthly parents to remedy mistakes from long ago. They would be free and so would I. I could receive everything I needed from my intimate connection with Papa God.

And so, I chose Jesus.

RESTORED

Out of this place of learning to be mothered and fathered by God, I have experienced restoration and wholeness. It is from my connection with Him and my position as His child, I interact in all my relationships. Motherhood has been another awakening journey. God has graciously used my seven children to call me deeper into Him.

Supernatural Mothering Ministries and this study were birthed out of my journey of being lost then found. It has been in His presence that I've been healed and transformed. The supernatural power of the cross and the Gospel are what have turned motherhood into a place of encounter and victory for me, rather than loneliness and defeat.

I know many of you can relate to my spiritual journey. Yet, you have your own precious story to share. My prayer is this study will invite you to embrace your own journey and meet Jesus at the intersection of your past and present. God has a divine appointment with you to know Him more as Father and Mother, to receive His unending love for you and to empower you to mother your children out of the fullness that comes from knowing Him.

WEEK ONE

Your Competence is From God

"It is not that we are competent in ourselves to consider anything as coming from ourselves, but our competence is from God."

2 Corinthians 3:5 HCSB

day one

"I can't do it! I'm not cut out for this!" How many times have I muttered this to the Lord as a mother of seven? "There was an old woman who lived in a shoe. She had so many children she didn't know what to do!" Sometimes I've found myself agreeing with the lie that like the old woman, I don't know how to adequately care for all my children.

Whether we have one or ten, motherhood is just more than we can handle. When we answered the "call" to motherhood, many of us didn't feel ready. We are not alone. God called others in the Bible, like Gideon and Moses, who didn't feel up to the task.

God-size tasks require God-size capabilities. When we surrender our own inadequacies and take on the sufficiency of Christ, we move from living in defeat as a mom to living in victory.

We no longer depend on our own adequacy to qualify us for the job. It is "Christ in me, the hope of glory" that we rely on to make us the moms He calls us to be (Colossians 1:27 ASV).

DAILY DECLARATION

I am a competent mother because I'm relying on Jesus to show me the way in everything I do today! I am up to the task! I can do this well with Jesus! I lay down my own limitations (*name any that come to mind*) and receive His limitless capabilities and resources to supernaturally mother my children through me today.

IN A NUTSHELL

Because Christ is in me, I am a competent, capable mother!

day two

READ & REFLECT

Write an honest, heart felt response to God's truth.

"I am the Vine, you are the branches. When you're joined with me and I with you, the relation intimate and organic, ***the harvest is sure to be abundant.*** *Separated, you can't produce a thing."*

John 15:5 The Message

- Intimate relationship with Jesus is the basis for abundance in every aspect of our life!

Are there areas in your life where you are trying to go it alone? Where do you need to invite Jesus to join you so you can thrive in motherhood, not just survive?

"But I will sing of your strength, in the morning I will sing of your love; for you are my fortress, my refuge in times of trouble. You are my strength, I sing praise to you; you, God, are my fortress, ***my God on whom I can rely.****"*

Psalm 59:16-17 NIV

- Because of who God is, we can rely on Him no matter what we are facing!

Can you echo the psalmist? Do you feel this has been God's track record with you? If so, how? If not, why?

"God will make this happen, for ***he who calls you is faithful.****"*

I Thessalonians 5:24 NLT

- God is 100% faithful! He has called you to be a mother. This is a privilege and enormous responsibility.

Do you trust Him to accomplish what you feel you can't? Why?

day three

HEART-TO-HEART WITH HOLY SPIRIT

Four miniature grocery carts go zooming down the aisle. I can be heard behind giving gentle correction. "Slow down! Say, 'Excuse me' to the lady on your left!" I'm just trying to grab a few groceries with seven kids in tow. They are enthusiastic helpers. But a simple trip for groceries can feel like a three-ring circus as we parade about the store.

Because it's unusual to see such a large family in our culture today, I get a variety of responses. A few dirty looks by those who feel I am single-handedly over-populating the world. A few smiles, mainly from the grandmothers, who look fondly at our brood with memories of their own. Out of my own insecurities, I used to take offense at those who judged my mothering. There is nothing as humbling as taking a tantruming two-year old out of the store while you're trying to maintain a shred of dignity. I would feel like a failure as I received judgmental glares. (I've learned now not to make any eye contact. Just put your head down and head for the nearest exit!)

But seriously, God's loving affirmation of our mothering must trumpet louder than any other voices. We need to hear and believe what He thinks about us in our role. We don't have to fear our own shortcomings. I find it is in the place of my own inadequacies and inabilities that I meet God most tangibly. The void is like a vacuum drawing in His presence. My weaknesses create a need for Him.

"Each time He said, 'My grace is all you need. My power works best in weakness. So now I am glad to boast about my weaknesses, so that the power of Christ can work through me. That's why I take pleasure in my weaknesses, and in the insults, hardships, persecutions, and troubles that I suffer for Christ. For when I am weak, then I am strong."

2 Corinthians 2:8-10 NLT

Your inadequacies are an invitation for a deeper encounter with His power! He welcomes you to exchange your weaknesses today for His power and strength.

What do you believe about your own abilities as a mother? Do you feel confident in your role?

ASK HOLY SPIRIT

"Is what I wrote down true about me?"

- Take a moment to listen to His response.
- If it is true, ask Him, *"What else do you want me to know about myself as a mother?"* God loves to heap extra encouragement onto truth we already believe. Move on to declaring these truths you wrote down out loud throughout the week (see Day Four).
- If it's not true, circle the lies you identify in your statements.

Break any agreements you've made with each lie.

Pray

"In the name of Jesus, I renounce the lie that I'm (*name the inadequacy*). I break any partnership I formed with this lie through my thoughts, attitudes, words or actions, known or unknown. I break the power of the lie and cancel its assignment against me."

Laugh at these lies (Psalm 2:2-4)**.**

In addition, lies are often tied to painful memories. To be free, it is crucial to forgive those who have wronged you and sown the seeds of this lie in your life.

Ask Holy Spirit

"Is there anyone I need to forgive for teaching me this lie?"

Pray

"I forgive (*name the person*) for (*name the offense*). I release (*name the person*) to you, Jesus. I ask that you bless (*name the person*). Jesus, please forgive me for believing the lie. Take the lie away and everything that came with it."

When I am still hurting over a situation, praying for God to bless the offender is often difficult for me. I long for justice, restitution, and reconciliation. But His Word reassures me it is His kindness that leads people to repentance (Romans 2:4). This prayer of forgiveness helps me totally surrender the situation to Him and align myself with His heart for others and for me.

WITH THE LIE & UNFORGIVENESS OUT OF THE WAY, ASK HOLY SPIRIT

"Please reveal to me the truth about my identity as a mom."

....

....

....

....

Pray

"Jesus, I take off (*name the weakness*) and put on Your (*name His strength, the opposite of your weakness*) in its place."

Speak to your spirit man and plant the truth He's revealed.

Declare

"I speak to my spirit that I am (*name the truths of who you are*). Thank you Jesus!"

day four

FAITH IN ACTION

Especially when we haven't had godly motherhood modeled, we can be confused about the way to live within this high calling. But God doesn't abandon us. The best way to learn how to mother our children is to allow God to mother us. He mothers us with His nurturing presence.

"When you see the ark of the covenant of the LORD your God,
and the Levitical priests carrying it
you are to move out from your positions and follow it.
Then you will know which way to go,
since you have never been this way before."

Joshua 3:3-4 NIV

The Israelites were crossing the Jordan river to enter the Promised Land. They hadn't been that way before. So God sent His Presence to go before them to lead the way.

God is so compassionate towards those who haven't been "this way" before. He is willing to intimately guide mothers as they raise their children up in the Lord (Isaiah 40:11). He commands us to teach our children to know and follow Him and therefore, equips us and shows us the way. He doesn't leave us powerless. Instead, He empowers us through Holy Spirit to do what He commands of us.

But we need to be willing to "move out from our positions," or old ways of thinking and doing things, that may hinder us from moving forward with Jesus.

What old ways of thinking or of doing things are holding you back?

Surrender these former ways at the feet of Jesus.

Pray

"Jesus, here are my old ways of thinking and doing things (*name them specifically*). I want to follow Your presence into a new and spacious place where I can experience the promised land – the complete adequacy and sufficiency of God for me and my family as I mother."

Turn the truths Holy Spirit revealed about your identity on Day Three into your own personal declarations. Write them on blank notecards.

- Place them where they will be readily visible to you today (*on your kitchen cabinet, bathroom mirror, car dashboard etc.*).
- Renew your mind by frequently declaring them out loud, especially when the enemy is trying to get you to believe the lie again.

Note: *If you find yourself meditating on an old mindset, go back to the prayer exercise on Day Three. Walk yourself through it again with Holy Spirit. Receive a new the truth about your identity.*

day five

STONES OF REMEMBRANCE JOURNAL

Record the manifestations of God's strength and power in areas where you feel weak. Describe what you have learned about His character as a result.

Pray

"Jesus, give me eyes to see and ears to hear your ever-present activity in my life. Help me to recognize your tangible strength and power in my times of trouble. Give me your perspective and show me how you are so reliable!"

WEEK TWO

The Power of Renewing Your Mind

"Do not conform to the pattern of this world,
but be transformed by the renewing of the mind..."

Romans 12:2 NIV

day one

Some years back, we went through a rough patch in our marriage. There wasn't one exact thing that was troubling us. Miscommunication, unforgiveness, and frustration were some of the weeds in our garden. I kept thinking and saying, "We don't have a good marriage."

One day, my husband pointed out this repetition to me. I wasn't aware I was continuously prophesying negativity over our marriage. At the time, I reasoned, there were simply things in our marriage I wanted changed or improved.

Eventually, by God's grace, I began thanking Him for a good marriage instead. I wasn't denying the problems we were facing, just confessing a better future. As a result, my perspective began to change. I began to focus more on the goodness of our marriage rather than on its shortcomings. I also began to hope and even expect more goodness would come.

Soon after, we joined a marriage ministry at our church. We learned some new tools for uprooting the weeds and preventing others from taking root. God's will is that we have a good marriage. I just started to agree with Him.

This change in my thinking helped unlock and prepare me for the creative solutions God had in store for us. Outward transformation starts with inward thinking.

DAILY DECLARATION

I am a transformed mother with God's Word accomplishing its purposes within me. My actions as a mother are washed and renewed by the Word of God. I am not stuck in old patterns or habits that try to hold me in bondage because God's Word always bears fruit. I align my thinking with the Word of God. I trust Him to bring about supernatural change in the way I respond to my husband and children today.

IN A NUTSHELL

I align my thinking with God's Word and receive His transformation!

day two

READ & REFLECT

Write an honest, heart felt response to God's truth.

"So My word that comes from My mouth ***will not return to me empty, but it will accomplish what I please and will prosper*** *in what I send it to do."*

Isaiah 55:11 HCSB

- God's Word is alive and active. It is filled with purpose to fulfill God's will in you and around you.

What Scriptures or prophetic words has God spoken to you that you need to pick up again and believe for their fulfillment in your life?

"For as he thinks in his heart, ***so he is.****"*

Proverbs 23:7 AMP

- What we think, we become. Our perspective bears its fruit in our circumstances. Pay attention to your thoughts.

What have you been mulling over lately? What statements are you repeating in your head? What kind of fruit do they bear?

"If you ***confess with your mouth*** *'Jesus is Lord' and* ***believe in your heart***
that God raised him from the dead, you will be saved.
One believes with the heart, resulting in righteousness,
and one confesses with the mouth, resulting in salvation."

Romans 10:9-10 HCSB

- What we say and believe are interconnected. Do you want to know what someone truly believes? Listen to their words.

"For the mouth speaks from the overflow of the heart."

Matthew 12:34 HCSB

In addition to paying attention to your thought life, listen to what you confess about yourself, others and your circumstances in conversation. Are your statements full of faith and hope? Or are they negative confessions?

Although this quote is not Scripture, it is loaded with God's truth and demonstrates the natural progression of our thought life to our destiny.

"Watch your thoughts, they become words.
Watch your words, they become actions.
Watch your actions, they become habits.
Watch your habits, they become your character.
Watch your character, it becomes your destiny."

www.orthodoxytoday.com

day three

HEART-TO-HEART WITH HOLY SPIRIT

We must sharpen our own perception. We may not always be aware of what we are thinking. We may be tossing around negative scenarios in our head under the guise of concern but it's really worry. From worry, we gain nothing good (Psalm 37:8 NIV).

Out of frustration or worry, we can make judgments that ultimately lead us down the wrong path. From a place of fear, I worried about our finances. Instead of confessing God's promises, I judged and blamed my husband. You can just imagine the negative fruit that bore! Under conviction of Holy Spirit, I became aware of my sin and my partnership with fear. Intentionally, when I saw my husband, I would quietly bless him, "You are a good and capable provider." This 180-degree turn in my thinking and confession altered my feelings towards him. My confidence in His abilities swelled as I saw him through Papa God's eyes.

ASK HOLY SPIRIT

"Please reveal to me any thoughts about myself, my husband, my children or my circumstances which are bearing negative fruit." (It could be an area you worry about, unresolved frustration, pain, or disappointment.)

Repent of agreeing with negative thoughts.

Pray

"In the name of Jesus, I renounce the lie (*name the negative thought*). I break any partnership I've formed with this lie through my thoughts, attitudes, words or actions, known or unknown. I break the power of the lie and cancel its assignment against me and anyone else involved."

Laugh at these lies (Psalm 2:2-4)**.**

Ask Holy Spirit

"Show me Your truth about this instead. How do you see (name the person or situation)? What is Your perspective?"

Note: *If you are having a hard time hearing the truth, it may be because the lie has been so deeply ingrained in your thinking. Seek out your husband, a friend, or your small group to help you discern God's perspective.*

Pray

"I bless (*name of person or situation*) with Your perfect will. (*Name the specific purposes you believe God has for this instead of the negative outcomes you've believed.*) Your Kindgom come, your will be done on earth, here in me and my situation, as it is in Heaven."

What new thoughts of truth do you need to start thinking, believing and confessing instead?

....

....

....

....

....

day four

FAITH IN ACTION

When old thought patterns rear their ugly heads this week, repent as you did on Day Three. Declare the truth He's showed you instead. This truth is God's perfect will and plan for you and your situation. Ask Holy Spirit to remind you when your thinking isn't in line with His.

Years ago, I was frequently having foreboding thoughts about our family's future. Subconsciously, I always anticipated the worst. If one of our children was sick, I'd assume it would develop into an asthma attack and require hospitalization. If finances were tight, I'd conclude we'd end up getting evicted.

When I became aware of these negative thoughts, I repented and broke agreements with the lies I believed about what was in store for us. Because this thought pattern had become so habitual, having been modeled in my family line for generations, it required a continual submission on my part to God's truth.

I had to break partnership with this lie repeatedly. Initially, I kept a copy of a similar prayer from Day Three within reach. When Holy Spirit reminded me I was thinking my old, foreboding thoughts again, I'd immediately repent and begin afresh with His truth.

Don't get discouraged if it takes several times of prayer and repentance before you establish habitual godly thinking! *Repent* means "to change one's mind and purpose," (*Dictionary of Words from the King James Bible*).

In *Igniting Faith in 40 Days*, Steve Backlund speaks of repentance like this, "It is important to repent *to* something, not just *from* something. It involves changing the mind from one course into a higher course" (Backlund 19). God has revealed to you a new way of thinking and empowered you to change your mind on the subject. You have deliberately started thinking His thoughts about it.

You were headed in one direction when you believed the lie. The truth has put you on a different course. You are now positioned toward a new purpose. Your new thoughts have set you up for Godly results.

As a fruit of your repentance, what new results are you now positioned to receive?

ASK HOLY SPIRIT

"What part do I play in bringing about these results?"

Quiet your heart. Commit to doing your part this week. Outline your plan of action below.

day five

STONES OF REMEMBRANCE JOURNAL

Steve Backlund says in *Igniting Faith in 40 Days,* "I set the course of my life today with my words" (James 3:2-5). (Backlund 42)

List evidence or fruit of your new thinking and the direction it establishes in your life.

Pray

"Jesus give me eyes to see and ears to hear Your truth. Help me to see how Your faithful word is bringing about transformation in me and around me."

WEEK THREE

The Strategic Mother

"Call to me and I will answer you.
I'll tell you marvelous and wonderful things
that you could never figure out on your own."

Jeremiah 33:3 The Message

day one

I was home puttering around the house. No one was there but me. I threw some laundry in the washer, scrubbed a few dishes, picked up some dirty clothes that had been left behind on the floor for the millionth time.

All the while I was tossing around in my head our need for a practical daily schedule. The chores weren't getting done. The time I wanted to spend in worship with the kids wasn't happening. Breakfast dishes remained on the table until lunch. I was desperate for a new way of doing things.

I laid my own hand on my head and imparted to myself a schedule from Heaven. There wasn't anyone else around to do it. I needed answers. So, I called on Holy Spirit within me and blessed myself with His wisdom and creativity.

Something happened. I felt His presence. A few minutes later, a wonderful idea of how to order my morning popped into my head!

It may seem rather silly to lay hands on oneself, but I was desperate for a fresh revelation for my family. The remarkable thing is that God was right there willing to powerfully impart to me what I had asked.

No, I wasn't asking for the cure for cancer or the secret to peace in the Middle East. It was simply a request for an effective, daily schedule for my family. God wants to reveal to us secrets of all kinds of magnitude. We just need to ask Him.

DAILY DECLARATION

I have been given strategies from Heaven for motherhood. God is with me. I call on Holy Spirit when I need help and He always answers me. Daily, I walk in His fresh revelation for me and my family.

IN A NUTSHELL

I have access to Heaven's strategies for supernatural motherhood!

day two

READ & REFLECT

Write an honest, heart felt response to God's truth.

*"Because **the secrets of the Kindgom of heaven have been given for you to know,** but it has not been given to them. **For whoever has, more will be given to him,** and he will have more than enough."*

Matthew 13:11-12 HCSB

- No matter how much revelation you've received, a lot or a little, it only means more is due your way.

What secrets of the Kindgom do you already know and live out in your home? Ask Holy Spirit for more revelation.

"Behold the virgin shall become pregnant and give birth to a Son,
and they shall call His name Emmanuel–which,
when translated, means, ***God with us.****"*

Matthew 1:23 AMP

- Emmanuel isn't just for Christmas. He's our everyday revelation of God's loving and intimate presence.

Where in your life, home and family do you tangibly sense God with you? In what areas do you need to cry out to Emmanuel and invite Him in?

"I will bless the Lord who has given me counsel; ***yes,***
my heart instructs me in the night seasons.*"*

Psalm 16:7 AMP

- God loves to speak to us through our nighttime dreams! Expect His instruction even in the night hours.

What has He been saying to you lately? How is He using your dreams to direct and guide you? Keep a record this week of your night dreams. If you are in a *Supernatural Mothering Small Group,* ***consider sharing these dreams with your group for further clarification and interpretation.***

day three

HEART-TO-HEART WITH HOLY SPIRIT

Read John 21:1-14.

The disciples went back to fishing after their hopes and dreams of Jesus reigning in Israel were dashed with His crucifixion. They were discouraged. It was the same old, same old again. Yet, Jesus appeared to them in the morning. He even initiated a fresh strategy for them, turning a fruitless trip into one overflowing with provision and adventure!

As a result, their eyes were opened. An even greater revelation for them took place. They recognized this kind of knowledge and insight could only have come from their Jesus!

When God shows us secrets of His Kindgom, He not only gives us new strategies for life. He also reveals to us more about Himself. Everything He does is to bring us into deeper intimacy with Him.

Do you need a fresh revelation and strategy for an area in your life that has become ho-hum? At times, aspects of motherhood and homemaking can feel mundane. Jesus can offer us strategies from Heaven, changing these difficult areas into grand adventures and places of abundance and encounter with Him.

What areas in your life need a new plan of action, a new approach, or fresh revelation?

To help you receive and hear God's specific strategies for these areas in your life, spend time waiting in His presence.

- Turn on soaking music to help you. Or, find a quiet place. You may even want to take a walk.
- Be still. Wait on Him until you hear His voice, see something He is showing you, or until someone comes banging on the door!

Spend time praying in tongues, your personal prayer language.

> *"For anyone who speaks in tongues does not speak to people but to God: indeed no one understands them; they utter mysteries by the Spirit."*
>
> I Corinthians 14:2 NIV

As you pray in tongues, Holy Spirit speaks revelation to your spirit. Sometimes, I walk around the house, going about my daily duties, quietly praying in tongues. I have found this especially helpful when I realize I'm worrying about a problem to which I have no solution yet.

Praying in tongues ministers faith and divine solutions to your spirit. Holy Spirit is speaking to you, solving the issue even before it is revealed to your mind.

Watch how God, with His supernatural presence and problem-solving, reveals the strategies you're seeking, often in a surprising way!

Note: *If you don't yet have a prayer language, reach out to your small group or your church leadership for a fresh baptism of Holy Spirit!*

> *"Now, if any of you lacks wisdom, he should ask God, who gives generously and without criticizing, and it will be given him."*
>
> James 1:5 HCSB

Spend time waiting in His presence and praying in tongues repeatedly throughout the week until you sense new strategies.

What new strategies has Holy Spirit revealed to you?

....

....

....

....

....

Receive and believe God is giving you an impartation of His wisdom. He gives an abundance of wisdom without ever finding fault in our lack.

Pray

"Jesus, thank you for Your wisdom, revelation and new strategies for me regarding (*name the area*)**.**"

day four

FAITH IN ACTION

By faith, lay hands on yourself.

This prophetic act is a step of agreement with Holy Spirit's impartation of wisdom (*or whatever you need for the situation*).

Otherwise, if you are doing this study in a small group setting, take time to lay hands on each other and impart what is needed. For example, someone in the group may be gifted in time management while someone else desperately needs help in this area. Impart the gift of time management and all that comes with it to the one seeking it.

To whoever has, more will be given. The Bible reminds us it will even be more than enough (Matthew 13:11-12)! The "more" often comes when we start giving away what we have to bless others.

Put the new strategies Holy Spirit showed you into place in your home and family life.

As you act on His revelation, you are partnering your faith with your works. Be faithful with what He has revealed. He will then meet you with more – more revelation and power to carry out these strategies.

What are the specific steps you will take to put new strategies into practice?

day five

STONES OF REMEMBRANCE JOURNAL

Record how God is meeting you with His presence and power to execute your new strategies.

Pray

"Jesus, give me eyes to see and ears to hear Your strategies. Help me to trust that when I call, You answer me and give me ideas I wouldn't have had without You. Show me how capable You are in meeting my need for fresh revelation in my mothering."

WEEK FOUR

Walking in Christ's Authority

"Look, I have given you the authority to trample on snakes and scorpions and over all the power of the enemy; nothing will ever harm you"

Luke 10:19 HCSB

day one

In one of my favorite children's books, *The Little White Horse*, the orphaned Maria finds a new home with her uncle at Moonacre Manor. Little does she know she is of a royal blood line.

It's a story of her journey towards her true identity as the Moon Princess who is predestined to one day save the valley from the Men of the Dark Woods. Slowly, she begins to walk in her authority, willingly submitting to the momentum of her destiny as the valley's deliverer. After she triumphs over the evil Monsieur Coq de Noir with her bravery, she insists he make friends with her family by inviting him to tea.

He submits saying, "Moon Maiden, I foresee that for the rest of my life I shall be obeying Your Highness' commands," and he agrees to come (Goudge 218). The tale ends with a feast where through Maria's strategic influence, relationships are restored and all ends in peace and happiness.

For years, I lived as the orphaned Maria. Because I was unaware of my true identity in

Christ, I didn't use the authority God had given me. I would experience oppression by the enemy or by sin and yet not reach for the powerful sword of the Spirit that already hung at my side. I couldn't very well use what I didn't know I had.

A mother's awareness of what she possesses in Christ is half the battle. If we are convinced we're weak or powerless to the obstacles and giants before us, we act like victims to our circumstances. But when we embrace our biblical position in Christ, nothing can stand in our way.

Just like with Maria, the enemy finds himself surrendering and obeying our biblical decrees because they carry with them the weight of God's authority. Although there is a battle to fight and at times it can be quite intense, Jesus promises, "Nothing will ever harm you" (Luke 10:19 HCSB). We live under His divine protection.

DAILY DECLARATION

I am a powerful mother who walks in the authority of Christ Jesus. I use my God-given authority to bring His Kindgom to rule and reign in my home, community, and nation. I have nothing to fear as I take up my authority against the schemes of the devil.

IN A NUTSHELL

I am a powerful mother wielding God's authority everywhere I go!

day two

READ & REFLECT

Write an honest, heart felt response to God's truth.

"Together with Christ Jesus He also raised us up and ***seated us in the heavens****…"*

Ephesians 2:6 HCSB

- We may be at the kitchen sink scrubbing breakfast dishes or cuddled up with little ones reading their favorite book. This is our position in the natural realm. However, in the spiritual realm, throughout our day, we rule and reign with Jesus in Heaven!

As you go about your day, how do you personally connect with your high position with Jesus?

"Have faith in God. I assure you: If anyone says to this mountain, 'Be lifted up and thrown into the sea,' and does not doubt in his heart but believes that what he says will happen, it will be done for him. Therefore I tell you, all the things you pray and ask for- ***believe that you have received them, and you will have them.****"*

Mark 11:22-24 HCSB

- When we pray, we must believe our prayers carry this kind of authority. We must take Jesus at His word.

What mountains in your life do you need to "speak to" with authority?

*"****For our battle is not against flesh and blood*** *but against the rulers, against the authorities, against the world powers of this darkness, against the spiritual forces of evil in the heavens."*

Ephesians 6:12 HCSB

- When we are in the throes of our day, it may be difficult to see beyond the spilled milk on the kitchen table. But we need to keep our spiritual awareness sharpened. We must be perceptive as to what is going on in the spiritual realm rather than just focusing on what is happening right before our natural eyes.

Are there any situations where natural solutions aren't bringing about the breakthrough you desire? Ask Holy Spirit to sharpen your spiritual vision in these areas. What does He want you to see is happening in the spiritual realm?

day three

HEART-TO-HEART WITH HOLY SPIRIT

Sibling rivalry was plaguing our house. With six boys, it constantly felt like someone was experiencing a degree of injustice or was the cause of it. One of my sons seemed to be continually provoking another. Strife was being stirred up right and left and I was at my wits' end.

The night before, my husband and I had entered into a discussion. As was typical, I became increasingly passionate about my point of view while he remained calm and listened. I said something to try to incite a more heated response from him and he replied, "Are you trying to provoke me?" I skirted around the issue and continued on with my plea.

The next day it hit me. This wasn't the first time I had used provocation as an argumentative tactic with my husband. "An angry man stirs up conflict" (Proverbs 29:22 HCSB). I was guilty of seeking to stir up conflict with my husband when I was feeling angry.

I realized I had been partnering with a provoking spirit. I had unleashed it in my own life and into our home. I knew as I dealt with this demonic spirit in my own life and broke its power over me through repentance and God's authority, I would break its power over my children as well.

As our awareness of the spiritual realm is heightened, we are able to walk more powerfully in our authority. We then know where to focus our efforts and trust God for full deliverance.

Are there any on-going, negative behaviors in your home?

ASK HOLY SPIRIT

"Show me the root cause of this behavior? Is there sin in my own life? Have I been partnering with a demonic spirit?"

Repent and ask His forgiveness.

Pray

"I nail (*name the sin, words or thoughts you're hearing*) to the cross. I break all agreements I've made with (*name the sin, words or thoughts you're hearing*) known or unknown and I repent of joining with (*name the sin, words or thoughts you're hearing*). I ask you, Father, to send (*name the sin, words or thoughts you're hearing*) away from me" (Byrne 10).

Ask Holy Spirit

What of His Kindgom and character does Holy Spirit want to give you in exchange for the sin or demonic spirit?

To help you, think of exchanging your sin for the opposite spirit. For example, God wants to fill us with His perfect love instead of fear since His "*Perfect love casts out fear*" (I John 4:18 NASB).

Pray

"Jesus, thank you for overcoming this sin for me on the cross. Fill me with Your spirit of *(name the opposite or what you desire)* instead of *(name the sin / demonic spirit)"* (Byrne 9).

Thank and praise Him for His deliverance and your new-found freedom!

Through your confession and the great exchange the cross of Jesus affords, you've just taken authority over sin and any demonic spirits you may have knowingly or unknowingly been partnering with in your home.

Use this prayer of repentance and deliverance with your children.

My oldest son (at age ten) was struggling with anger. I offered to pray with him so he could give his anger to Jesus. He wasn't ready. Later, I approached him and gently cautioned him against hardening His heart to the Lord. He was feeling discouraged because he felt he had asked Jesus for help but wasn't experiencing His immediate deliverance. His heart was growing angry and offended with God.

Later, my third son (at age six) threw an angry fit. I sent him to his room to calm down. When he came out, he apologized to me and I offered to pray with him. I led him through a version of the prayer. I had him repeat each line after me. A smile returned to his face. The weight of sin was gone!

Little did I know my oldest son was watching us. He said, "Mom, I want you to pray with me too." Thank you Holy Spirit for working in his heart!

If the child is young: Simplify the prayer's wording to make it age-appropriate. Have them repeat each phrase after you.

If the child is older: This prayer is especially powerful when the child comes under personal conviction by Holy Spirit. Their hearts are better prepared for repentance if Holy Spirit Himself convicts them of their need for forgiveness and deliverance. Pray and trust this will happen.

Otherwise, ask Holy Spirit how to help you gently present this without condemnation. With gentle guidance, you can help point out the sin and lead them through the prayer.

Our children are on a spiritual journey just like us. Sometimes, they need us to give them freedom for it to be a messy process. We need to give Jesus room to work in their hearts. He is so faithful! We just need to trust Him and be patient!

day four

FAITH IN ACTION

A great starting place for walking in your God-given authority is to know and believe what God says about you and your inheritance. Meditate on the following verses about your authority and your true position in Christ. Embrace your identity in Jesus and allow His truth to penetrate you to your very core.

"Faith comes by hearing..." (Romans 10:17 NIV). So, frequently read these Scriptures. Read them aloud. Believe them. Receive them. Renew your mind with them! As you are inwardly renewed, you will experience outward transformation (Romans 12:2).

Read the following verses. Summarize what God says about your identity.

To personalize their message, insert your own name where appropriate. Read various versions of the passage to allow your spirit man to hear them afresh.

Ephesians 1:3-14

Romans 8:14-17

Isaiah 61:1-4

These are God's intimate thoughts about you.

Turn these summaries into your own personal declarations. Write them on blank notecards.

Release and impart through declarations and the laying on of hands this godly inheritance over your family as well.

day five

STONES OF REMEMBRANCE JOURNAL

Record the new fruit your personal deliverance is bearing in your life and in your family's life.

Pray

"Jesus give me eyes to see and ears to hear. Help me to recognize and receive the victories You won for me on the cross. Give me discernment as I take up Your authority in the spirit realm."

WEEK FIVE

Freedom from Generational Sin

"Christ redeemed us from that self-defeating, cursed life by absorbing it completely into himself. Do you remember the Scripture that says, 'Cursed is everyone who hangs on a tree'? That is what happened when Jesus was nailed to the Cross: He became a curse, and at the same time dissolved the curse."

Galatians 3:13 The Message

day one

As a little girl, I had horrific nightmares. What made them so frightening was I could feel them coming on before I even went to sleep. Even when I'd wake up from one, the nightmare experience didn't end. The distortions were still there even when my eyes were open. My mom and my grandmother suffered similar nightmares. Although I didn't know the exact details of their experiences, I knew the door to the demonic had been opened through my family line..

I stopped having these nightmares before my teen years. Yet the night hours were still a scary time for me. When I became a mother, I wanted to ensure these nightmares wouldn't pass on to my own children. When my first-born was just a baby, I prayed and believed the nightmares no longer had any power and repented from the sin of fear. None of my seven children have ever experienced repetitive nightmares like I did when I was a child!

Praise God! The generational sin stopped with me! Successive generations will not have to suffer under it. Thank you Jesus for the cross!

When we find it difficult to break out of old habits or mindsets, even with our best effort, we might discover a generational sin is at play. Even after reading numerous "how to" books, setting goals, and at times, successfully changing our actions, we may still feel a strong compulsion towards the opposite direction of what we are trying to achieve.

But just because sin is modeled and passed down doesn't mean it has to be passed on! What we find on the other side of the cross is every spiritual blessing- our new spiritual heritage! It is not humanly possible to bring about significant change and transformation in our lives on our own. We need the power of Jesus to set us free supernaturally.

DAILY DECLARATION

I am a redeemed mother because no generational sin or demonic influence has power over me. I am no longer bound by the limitations of my natural family line. I am Papa God's daughter. Jesus is Lord over me, my husband, and my children. I am reaping every spiritual blessing because He became a curse in my place.

IN A NUTSHELL

God set me free from generational sin and now I have access to every spiritual blessing!

day two

READ & REFLECT

Write an honest, heart felt response to God's truth.

"If the Son sets you free, ***you really will be free.****"*

John 8:36 HCSB

- Jesus secured complete freedom for us and our children on the cross.

Are you currently experiencing total freedom? Why or why not? In what areas do you want to experience more of God's freedom?

*"**God sent him to buy freedom for us** who were slaves to the law, **so that he could adopt us as his very own children**. And because we are his children, God has sent the Spirit of his Son into our hearts, prompting us to call out, 'Abba, Father.'"*

Galatians 4:5-6 NLT

- Our freedom was purchased with His blood. Through the cross, we have been adopted into a new family line, the line of Jesus Christ. This is a family line void of sin and overflowing with blessings.

Which spiritual blessings would you especially like to see manifested in your family line? (To help you, think about the things Satan has tried to rob from you and your family through generations.)

The spiritual blessings you've listed are what God has for you in your new family line in Christ Jesus! Thank Jesus for purchasing these blessings for you on the cross!

*"So, you too consider yourselves **dead to sin but alive to God** in Christ Jesus."*

Romans 6:11 HCSB

- You are dead to the sin in your family line. Because you have been born again, your spirit now responds and is alive to God.

In what ways do you want your spirit to be more responsive to the things of God?

day three

HEART-TO-HEART WITH HOLY SPIRIT

Take your place as a powerful mother and stand in your God-given authority. Armed with the truth of Christ, you can cancel any generational sin's hold in your life, the lives of your children and all the generations to follow. It's time to break free from generational sins and enjoy the fullness of your blessed inheritance in Christ Jesus.

ASK HOLY SPIRIT

"Show me any stronghold in my life that has its roots in a generational sin."

Pray

"I forgive (*name the forefather*) for (*name the sin and how it has affected you*). I repent of any ways I've joined with, acted out or agreed with (*name the sin*) knowingly or unknowingly.

I place the cross of Jesus in my blood line, between me and (*name the forefather*), a thousand generations back and a thousand generations forward. I nail (*name the sin*) to the cross. I renounce this ungodly part of my natural heritage and I receive my spiritual heritage in Christ.

In the name of Jesus, I take authority over (*name the sin*) and I command its power in my life to be broken now. In the name of Jesus, I command all demon spirits associated with (*name the sin*) to leave me, my spouse and our children now. Jesus, wash me with your blood.

In the place of (*name the sin*), I release and receive (*name the opposite*). Thank you Jesus!" (Byrne 5)

After we repent and break the generational sin in our life, Jesus teaches us to fill its place so that the demonic will not return once again with oppression (Luke 11:24-26). This is why it is important to release and receive the opposite. The cross is the place of the great exchange! You can apply this exchange at the cross to every area of your life.

By praying the prayer above, you are confessing and appropriating the finished work of the cross into your life. You confessed you are dead to your natural heritage but are alive anew in Christ! Jesus is Lord over you and your family. He is master, not the generational sin.

Record what you released and received in place of the generational sin. This is your new spiritual heritage in Christ! Grab onto it! It's a new day in Him!

FAITH IN ACTION

Wake up to your new day and new heritage in Jesus! Before Jesus gave up His spirit on the cross, He spoke the words, "It is finished" (John 19:30 HCSB). The cross was a complete work, lacking nothing. Every curse was broken, every sickness and disease carried, and every sin atoned for. For you, with this generational sin, it is finished. It stops here by the blood of Jesus.

If you had just inherited a billion dollars, it would take some time for this reality to sink in. Your surroundings would still look the same. The next morning, you'd wake up and put on the same bathrobe. You'd drink your coffee out of the same mug. You might feel the same. But the difference would be someone had just deposited a billion dollars into your bank account.

Soon after, it's likely you'd start dreaming and planning where and how to spend your new inheritance. Your lifestyle would gradually begin to change, as you started withdrawing from the new wealth you had been given. You might even buy a new bathrobe to wear!

The same event occurred when you repented of the generational sin. By doing so, you broke open a pathway for your Godly inheritance in an area, which was previously blocked by a stronghold.

"One who breaks open the way will advance before them; they will break out,
pass through the gate, and leave by it.
Their King will pass through before them, the Lord as their leader."

Micah 2:13 HCSB

The Lord Jesus broke open the way on the cross. The King is leading you out of bondage through His deliverance. He is your leader. In turn, you are leading successive generations to freedom as well!

Things around you might look the same and feel the same. However, because you know what has been released, received and deposited within you, it's time to start your spending spree! You can draw on this new inheritance anytime you need it! Go ahead! You're rich! You can even take the liberty to spread it around to others everywhere you go!

Note: *When the bondage of sin tries to creep its way back into your life, pray the prayer from Day Three over again. Continue applying the blood of Jesus and the finished work of the cross to your family line. Be persistent. You may have to do this numerous times. Let that prayer be your immediate response when you come face-to-face with the generational sin again. Continue to release and receive the opposite.*

ASK HOLY SPIRIT

"Please show me more about my new heritage in Jesus. Lead me to scripture verses about (name the areas you've released and received) that I can stand on!"

List two or three Scriptures reinforcing this specific portion of your inheritance.

These Scriptures now serve as the sword of the Spirit and the shield of faith against the flaming arrows of the devil for you in this battle (Ephesians 6:16-17). Use them as offensive and defensive weapons!

When you are tempted to revert back to that sinful habit, confess those Scriptures. They will release God's Word, alive and active, into your life so it will bear the fruit you and He both desire.

As the rain and the snow come down from heaven,
and do not return to it without watering the earth and making it bud and flourish,
so that it yields seed for the sower and bread for the eater,
so is my word that goes out from my mouth:
It will not return to me empty,
but will accomplish what I desire and achieve the purpose for which I sent it.

Isaiah 55:10-11 NIV

day five

STONES OF REMEMBRANCE JOURNAL

Watch for evidence of your new heritage, taking root in the soil of your life!

"Behold, I am doing a new thing!
Now it springs forth; do you not perceive and know and will you not give heed to it?
I will even make a way in the wilderness and rivers in the desert."

Isaiah 43:19 AMP

Record the seedlings of new beginnings springing forth as a result of your prayer, belief and persistent stand on God's Word.

Pray

"Jesus, give me eyes to see and ears to hear the new beginnings, regardless of how small. Daily, help me to choose to side with my new inheritance of spiritual blessings rather than wallow in the past. I put my hope in You."

WEEK FIVE

WEEK SIX

The Peaceful Mother

"You will keep in perfect peace, all who trust in you, all whose thoughts are fixed on you!"

Isaiah 26:3 NLT

day one

"I think I'm in labor!" Normally, this is an exciting, joyous announcement. However, I was 30 weeks pregnant with twins. The thought of pre-term labor was frightening. After an emergency trip to the hospital, my contractions did subside. But I was "sentenced" to full bed rest. Not an easy feat for a woman with three other children under the age of six!

While on bed rest, a dear intercessor from our church came and visited me. I told her how I desperately needed more peace. She reminded me I had the Prince of Peace (in Hebrew, Sar shalom) living fully inside of me. Therefore, I had all the peace I needed. All I had to do was receive His peace and release it over myself and my unborn babies.

Not only was I fighting a physical battle to keep my babies in my womb, but I was fighting a battle in my mind as well. Fear wanted to consume my every thought about the babies. But I had a choice.

I could meditate on all the "what if's" and read in my "twin books" about all the horrible complications that could result if I gave birth early. Or, I could meditate on Jesus, His love for my babies, His ability to guard them and keep them and His perfect plan for their birth.

To keep my mind fixed on Jesus, I posted Scriptures on the wall near my bed as reminders of His promises to me and the twins. When a fearful thought would come, I would take it captive by confronting the lie that fear was spouting with the truth of these Scriptures. It was amazing to experience the victory and freedom that came from believing and declaring God's Word!

At 35 weeks, I gave birth to two perfectly healthy, beautiful boys, Joseph and Stephen. God miraculously kept me and those babies in His perfect peace.

DAILY DECLARATION

I am a peaceful mother. I am focused on Jesus, not the difficulties or uncertainties. I trust Jesus with all things, at all times. The Prince of Peace lives in me and fills me. I release His peace to my mind, my body, my husband and my marriage, my children and my home. I command any storms raging, "Peace be still!"

IN A NUTSHELL

I am a peaceful mother because the Prince of Peace lives within me!

day two

READ & REFLECT

Write an honest, heart felt response to God's truth.

*"**Of the increase of His government and of peace there shall be no end,** upon the throne of David and over his Kindgom, **to establish it and to uphold it** with justice and with righteousness from the (latter) time forth, even forevermore. **The zeal of the Lord of hosts will perform this.**"*

Isaiah 9:7 AMP

- God's order (government) and peace is ever increasing on the earth! It is ever increasing in you and your home as well!

In fact, peace is a fruit of order. Think about the relationship between order and peace in your own life. What correlations do you see?

"Yahweh your God is among you, a warrior who saves.
He will rejoice over you with gladness.
He will bring you quietness with His love.
He will delight in you with shouts of joy."

Zephaniah 3:17 HCSB

- Let Him quiet the storms in your heart today with His love.

Write a prayer inviting Jesus to pour His love on you in the places where you may be experiencing turmoil or difficulty. Take a moment to receive His extravagant love for you. In order to help you anticipate receiving from the Father, position yourself physically by opening your hands to Heaven. Enjoy His quiet peace that follows.

"Turn away from evil and do what is good; ***seek peace and pursue it.****"*

Psalm 34:14 HCSB

- The Bible tells us to pursue peace. The *Collins English Dictionary* defines *pursue* as: "to follow in order to overtake, capture, or chase." Remember: Peace is a person, Jesus Christ!

Do you currently find yourself in a place of peace? How can you start or continue to pursue peace within your circumstances? Ask Holy Spirit to show you the way.

day three

HEART-TO-HEART WITH HOLY SPIRIT

There was a season when we struggled financially, living on part-time incomes. Financial lack would spring up and try to rock my boat. If I focused on it, I'd find myself worried, joyless and even snappy with my husband and kids. So instead, I tried to return to my point of reference for peace.

My point of reference for peace is His presence and who He is, not what I may be temporarily experiencing. So during that season, I would thank Jesus for who He was in the midst of my financial storm. I would declare His faithful character over the situation, verbally or through worship, to remind myself of the greater Truth at play. My circumstances do shift, but God is unchanging.

An awareness of the paths you tend to take towards or away from peace will encourage you to intentionally choose peace at all times.

What is your personal way to peace and your susceptibility away from peace?

According to Isaiah 9:7 (Day Two's Scripture), peace and order are part of a Kindgom's sure foundation. They are part of the foundation of a well-established life and home as well.

Is there anything hindering peace from prevailing in your life and in your home? Are there areas out of order in your family?

Give Papa God your obstacles to peace.

Offer Him any out-of-order family relationships or priorities. Release to Him any other areas of disorder.

Pray

"Jesus, I bring *(name the area)* to the foot of your cross. I leave *(name the area)* there and entrust it to you. I have held tightly to it because it has offered me an illusion of peace and control. I no longer want it or need it. I choose You.

In the place of** (name the area)**, what do You have for me?"

Pray

"Thank you Jesus for *(name what Jesus gave you in its place).* I love you!"

Choose one of these well-known hymns to sing. Sing or say it as a prayer. Let it's truth minister to your spirit.

My Hope is Built on Nothing Less *by Edward Mote, 1834*

My hope is built on nothing less, Than Jesus' blood and righteousness;
I dare not trust the sweetest frame, But wholly lean on Jesus' name.
On Christ, the solid Rock, I stand; All other ground is sinking sand.
All other ground is sinking sand.

Turn Your Eyes Upon Jesus *by Helen H. Lemmel, 1922*

O soul, are you weary and troubled? No light in the darkness you see?
There's a light for a look at the Savior, And life more abundant and free!
Turn your eyes upon Jesus, Look full in His wonderful face,
And the things of earth will grow strangely dim, In the light of His glory and grace.

day four

FAITH IN ACTION

This week, when you need peace and are seeking it, don't look outwardly. Instead, turn to the Shalom of God within you. Turning inwardly doesn't mean relying on your own resources. Instead, you are looking to the deposit of peace Holy Spirit has placed within you! Peace is the fruit of His Spirit living inside of you (Galatians 5:22).

The literal translation for *peace* is "shalom." This Hebrew word has a much fuller definition than our English understanding of *peace*. According to *Strong's Concordance* 7965 *Shalom* means "completeness, wholeness, health, peace, welfare, safety, soundness, tranquility, prosperity, perfectness, fullness, rest, harmony, the absence of agitation or discord."

One Hebrew scholar translates it as "No good thing is withheld." *Shalom* seems to sum up much of the blessings and inheritance God wants to pour into our lives!

Jesus said, "My peace (*shalom*) I leave you. My peace (*shalom*) I give to you. I do not give to you as the world gives. Do not let your hearts be troubled and do not be afraid" (John 14:27 HCSB).

The Message Bible says it like this: "I'm leaving you well and whole. That's my parting gift to you. Peace (*Shalom*). I don't leave you the way you are used to being left – feeling abandoned, bereft. So don't be upset. Don't be distraught" (John 14:27 The Message).

You can call yourself a peaceful mother because the Giver of every good gift has left His Shalom for you to daily receive and experience! Believe you have peace even before you may fully experience it. Believing by faith is a crucial step towards experience.

Numbers 6:22-26 is a powerful priestly blessing I love to pray over my children and to receive for myself as well. In Old Testament times, this blessing was only proclaimed by the priests. Today, by the death and resurrection of Jesus, you and I are of the holy priesthood and have now been given authority through Jesus to declare this over others (I Peter 2:9)!

Take time this week to proclaim these verses over yourself, your husband and each of your children. This is God's heart for you! Instead of "you," insert the person's name.

Pray

"The Lord will bless you and He will keep you. The Lord will make His face to shine upon you and He will be gracious to you. The Lord will lift His countenance to you and He will establish Shalom for you."

Numbers 6:22-26 One New Man Bible

Shalom is not something for which you strive. Trust Him to set you in His Shalom. Let Him establish Shalom in you and around you. It is His gift and His will for you in Christ Jesus! He is passionate about seeing you and your children steeped in His Shalom!

day five

STONES OF REMEMBRANCE JOURNAL

Record the Shalom of God that you recognize in your own life and your home! Thank Jesus for His gift! It is ever-increasing in you. Expect more!

Pray

"Jesus, give me eyes to see and ears to hear Your Shalom. Raise my awareness of the Shalom you've graciously woven into the fabric of my days. I receive and choose Your peace."

WEEK SEVEN

Entering His Rest

"Come to Me, all you who are weary and burdened, and I will give you rest.
All of you, take up My yoke and learn from Me,
because I am gentle and humble in heart, and you will find rest for yourselves.
For My yoke is easy and My burden is light."

Matthew 11:28-30 HCSB

day one

Nine weeks before giving birth to our seventh baby, my husband was applying for a job as a children's pastor in various states around the country. My nesting hormones were kicking in and I didn't even know exactly where I'd be giving birth.

With anxiety about having a newborn in the midst of such uncertainty, I implored my husband, "We need a future." He looked at me with his ever-steady eyes and said, "We have a future." I knew what he said was true. Jesus is our future. He's our everything.

But my spirit cried, "I need a place to lay my head." I didn't mean physically. We had a house we had made into a home. I needed a place to rest. Aaria, in the *Spirit of the King*, had this same need. Recently rescued from bondage to a dark kindgom, the King brings Aaria into a new land.

"Exhausted, Aaria sank to the ground beside him (the King). Neither spoke a word as he knelt down and cared for her needs, feeding her starved frame. He then pulled back the flap on the small tent prepared for her, and she lay down and slept. The firelight cast his silhouette up onto the tent entrance. It remained there, swaying from the shifting light of the flickering flames as he guarded her, his supernatural presence warding off movements that approached the camp throughout the night" (Hay 8).

There is a time to stand and fight, and a time to rest. Both can accomplish the same victory. We just need His discernment to know which position to take and when.

Resting seems easier and far more intimate. Weary, you crawl up into Papa God's lap. Your armor lies at His feet. You curl up and fall asleep. Someone else is in charge — Jesus. No words need to be spoken between you. You trust Him to meet all your needs, to protect you in times of trouble, to care for all that concerns you. You rest.

DAILY DECLARATION

I am a restful mother. I don't spin my wheels endlessly in hopes my world doesn't crumble. Instead, I trust the Maker of Heaven and earth to carry and make right all things that concern me. I rest in His goodness and faithfulness to me. My life is carefree and secure under the shadow of His wings.

IN A NUTSHELL

I am resting in His caring, capable arms!

day two

READ & REFLECT

Write an honest, heart felt response to God's truth.

*"**Cease striving** and know that I am God."*

Psalm 46:10 NASB

- Resting means knowing and trusting in the great I AM! It is in a place of rest, not of striving, where we also experience His restoration (Psalm 23:2-3).

Are there areas you are striving to make right and bring to completion on your own?

....

....

....

ASK HOLY SPIRIT

"What do you want to reveal to me about Yourself and Your heart for me in this situation?"

"Is there a lie I am believing about who You are that is preventing me from fully entering Your rest?"

Break any agreements you've made with each lie.

Pray

"In the name of Jesus, I renounce the lie that You are (*name the characteristic*). I break any partnership I formed with this lie through my thoughts, attitudes, words or actions, known or unknown. I break the power of the lie and cancel its assignment against me."

Laugh at these lies (Psalm 2:2-4)**.**

Ask Holy Spirit

"Is there anyone I need to forgive for teaching me this lie?"

Pray

"I forgive *(name the person)* for *(name the offense)*. I release *(name the person)* to You, Jesus. I ask that you bless *(name the person)*. Jesus, please forgive me for believing the lie. Take the lie away and everything that came with it. "

WITH THE LIE & UNFORGIVENESS OUT OF THE WAY, ASK HOLY SPIRIT

"In order to help me rest in who You are, what part of Your character do I need to get to know better? Please reveal to me the truth about who You are."

"The generous will prosper; ***those who refresh others will themselves be refreshed.****"*

Proverbs 11:25 NLT

- In the midst of all the cleaning, diaper changing, tying shoes, car-pooling, etc., God has promised you refreshment. In our place of service as mothers, one way refreshment comes is as we pour ourselves out to refresh others!

Who will you intentionally "refresh" today? As you do, believe His promise to refresh you as well!

"Walk with me and work with me — ***watch how I do it.***

Learn the "unforced rhythms of grace."

I won't lay anything heavy or ill-fitting on you.

Keep company with me and you'll learn to live freely and lightly."

Matthew 11:28-30 The Message

What "unforced rhythms of grace" have you already learned in your life? Where are you living freely and lightly? In what areas would you like Holy Spirit to reveal new "unforced rhythms of grace?"

Pray

"I welcome your *unforced rhythms of grace* in my life, Jesus. Come Holy Spirit."

day three

HEART-TO-HEART WITH HOLY SPIRIT

It is difficult to rest when you are carrying burdens God never intended you to carry. When I begin to feel overwhelmed with what is on my plate, it is often because I have taken on a helping that doesn't belong to me. Here's a test: Jesus says, "My yoke is easy and My burden is light" (Matthew 11:30 HCSB) .

Do you feel motherhood is a constant hardship and you feel weighed down by it? Or, despite the daily demands on you, is your step light and your way easy?

ASK HOLY SPIRIT

"Which burdens are mine and which belong to someone else? Please give me Your discernment to know the difference."

Concerning the load that does belongs to you, Jesus wants to share it with you. "Blessed be the Lord, Who bears our burdens and carries us day by day, even the God who is our salvation!" (Psalm 68:19 AMP).

Take a moment to hand Him, verbally and physically, all the burdens you are carrying.

Picture Him supporting the weight you once carried on His strong, capable shoulders. Climb into His arms and let Him carry you as well, day by day, hour by hour.

Pray

"Jesus, here is (*name the burden*). Please carry it for me and take care of everything that concerns me."

Jesus exhorts, "All of you, take up My yoke and learn from me, because I am gentle and humble in heart and you will find rest for yourselves" (Matthew 11: 29 HCSB).

A yoke speaks of partnership. The *Collins English Dictionary* defines *yoke* as "a wooden frame...for attaching to the necks of a pair of draught animals...so that they can be worked as a team." He wants to share the work with you. You were never intended to live out motherhood alone. He wants to team up with you!

Ask Holy Spirit

"How do you want to team up with me in (list a situation that concerns you)?"

Now receive His partnership. Thank Him for what He will do on your behalf. When you find yourself trying to do it alone again, climb back up into His lap and link arms with Jesus.

It is from a place of rest and partnership rather than striving and self-reliance that we experience being "more than conquerors in Christ Jesus and gain a surpassing victory through Him who loved us" (Romans 8:37 AMP).

day four

FAITH IN ACTION

Let's get practical! How do mothers enter and remain in a place of rest with Jesus when there is always so much to be done?

1. Refresh Others

I know this seems like an oxymoron. But isn't that just like the Kindgom? Because a mother's life is a continual act of service, isn't it wonderful to know as we serve others, God promises to refresh our spirits as well?

While you are serving, connect with Papa God. Acknowledge His presence with you and thank Him by faith that as you refresh your family, you yourself will be refreshed (Proverbs 11:25 NLT).

Remember: This doesn't mean to over-extend yourself without utilizing other opportunities for rest. It's not the only place of refreshment, but it can be found here.

2. Take a Temporary Rest

The Greek word *anapausis* means "temporary rest." This is the rest Jesus speaks of in Matthew 11:28 where He says, "I will give you rest." Give yourself a break. Jesus wants to give you rest.

Regular breaks prevent burnout. There are times I'll be in tears at the end of a day over little things and wonder what is going on with me. Often, I can trace it back to the fact I haven't taken a true break in a few days. This is not a sustainable model for motherhood!

Set aside short breaks for yourself during your busy day. Start your morning or end your day spending time with Jesus. Close the door to your bedroom, light a candle, and pick up a good book while your children are resting or playing in the backyard. Go out to coffee with a friend.

Shed condemnation. Receive what Jesus wants to give you — a temporary rest from your labor. You have His permission. He loves you so much!

3. Pray in Tongues

"For with stammering lips and another tongue will he speak to this people. To whom he said, This is the rest wherewith ye may cause the weary to rest; and this is the refreshing: yet they would not hear."

Isaiah 28:11-12 KJV

Praying in tongues is instrumental in remaining and maintaining a position of rest. Use it when you need to rest physically, but for various reasons you can't. Let Holy Spirit minister to your spirit as you go about your tasks, praying in tongues.

Also, pray in tongues when anxiety or spiritual warfare is at large in your life. At these times, you may struggle to enter His rest. Tongues can forge a path for you through the darkness into a place of resting with Jesus. It's another way to deliberately partner with Him!

Set aside three days to put each mode of rest into practice, one each day. Record your experiences. When you feel weary, intentionally implement one form of rest. I pray all three will become life-giving habits to take you from weariness to rest!

Date: ____________________ Refreshing others while receiving His promised refreshment

....

....

....

Date: ____________________ Setting time apart for temporary rest

....

....

....

Date: ____________________ Praying in tongues when you need to experience His rest

....

....

....

day five

STONES OF REMEMBRANCE JOURNAL

"Rest in the Lord and wait patiently for Him."

Psalm 37:7 One New Man Bible

Record the new "unforced rhythms of grace" Holy Spirit is teaching you.

Pray

"Jesus, give me eyes to see and ears to hear Your invitations to rest. Help me to recognize where I am striving and to walk with You in your light and easy ways instead."

WEEK EIGHT

Everything You Need

"Jesus has the power of God, by which he has given us everything we need to live and to serve God. We have these things because we know him. Jesus called us by his glory and goodness."

2 Peter 1:3 NCV

day one

When my twins were newborns, I was exhausted. I nursed them every one and a half hours around the clock for the first few months. My other three little boys (under age six) still needed time and attention from mom. I gave it but it didn't seem to be enough. Daily, I was physically and emotionally rung dry like a sponge.

During this time, God really spoke to me through 2 Kings 4:1-7. My Bible summarizes it as "The Miracle of the Oil." A widow is in debt and the creditors are threatening to sell her children into slavery. She cries out to Elisha for help. He instructs her to gather empty vessels from her neighbors and pour into them her last jar of oil, her only possession of value. He tells her "do not get few," but wants her to have many so she can fill them full and sell them to pay off her debts. The Lord said to me, "These vessels are your children." I only had a small jar of oil (my current capabilities) and many little vessels to fill under my roof. Our children's capacity and needs often far outreach what we have to give. But God wants to do a miracle in our house!

He wants us to give our all, holding nothing back. When we've poured it all out, He will multiply what we have given and make it enough! He will fill our children completely with what they need! Remarkably, in this miracle, the oil only stopped multiplying when there were no more vessels to fill.

This revelation brought me great freedom. I am not solely responsible for my children's needs nor does God want me to be able to meet all of them. He desires each of us to need Him intimately. He wants our children to learn from an early age that He is "El-Shaddai" the all-sufficient one. Mom isn't! Daily, we give our children our best, trusting God to multiply our efforts and make up the difference.

DAILY DECLARATION

I have a close, intimate relationship with Jesus. Everything I need today flows out of my knowing Him. He fulfills all things. His faithful track record reassures me that no matter what I face, I do not lack anything I need. He delights in helping me. He is pleased when I ask.

IN A NUTSHELL

Because I know Him personally, I have everything I need!

day two

READ & REFLECT

Write an honest, heart felt response to God's truth.

"The Lord is my shepherd, ***there is nothing I lack...***
You prepare a table before me in the presence of my enemies;
You anoint my head with oil; ***My cup overflows.****"*

Psalm 23:1, 5 HCSB

- What a picture of God's awesome provision in the midst of David's weariness, darkness, and adversity! No matter what enemies you may be facing today (lack, fear, strife etc.), God has prepared a feast of His presence in their midst.

Let Jesus anoint you today with the oil of His Holy Spirit for the tasks and challenges ahead. He wants to overflow your cup. The *American Heritage College Dictionary* defines *overflow* as "to be filled beyond capacity and to have a boundless supply."

In the Middle East, it was a common practice to anoint one's visitors with a very fragrant perfume and to give them a cup of choice wine. The host was careful to fill the cup until it overflowed. The perfume was a demonstration of their love and respect; the overflowing cup of wine implied the visitors would have an abundance of everything while they were under their roof. There is an abundance of everything at our disposal because we are in Jesus' loving care!

Read all of Psalm 23.

Which verse particularly speaks to you? Write the verse below, inserting your name where appropriate. Declare this over your life.

"How excellent is Your loving kindness, O God! Therefore,
the children of men put their trust under the shadow of Your wings.
They will be abundantly satisfied with the fatness of Your House and
You will make them drink from the river of Your pleasures."

Psalm 36:8-9 One New Man Bible

- Under Jesus' care and protection, we experience true satisfaction. He doesn't satisfy us with leftovers but with the fatness of His house and quenches our thirst from the river of His pleasures.

Are you looking somewhere else other than to Jesus to be abundantly satisfied? Where?

ASK HOLY SPIRIT

"What is in the fatness of Your House and in the river of Your pleasures for me?"

*"**Taste and see that the Lord is good.** How happy is the man who takes refuge in Him! You, who are His holy ones, fear Yahweh, **for those who fear Him lack nothing.** Young lions lack food and go hungry, **but those who seek the Lord will not lack any good thing.**"*

Psalm 34:8-10 HCSB

- You are seeking Him. Therefore, you do not lack any good thing! Period.

However, in what areas of your life are you experiencing any lack?

Lack is a demonic spirit. It is contrary to the very nature of God. Speak this promise of not lacking any good thing over that area.

Declare

"Jesus, I am seeking You. Therefore I will not lack *(name the area).*"

This week, commit to focusing on His goodness not on the lack.

Despite the lack you may feel, what is the manifest goodness of God for you in this area?

HEART-TO-HEART WITH HOLY SPIRIT

In the English Bible, the Hebrew word, El Shaddai is translated "Almighty." *El* means powerful, almighty, eternal God. *Shaddai* comes from the root word "shad," which is the Hebrew word for breast. It literally means "the breasted one" (Campbell 5).

God intends for all of us to first encounter Himself in the natural as El Shaddai at our mother's breast. The breastfeeding relationship is a powerful representation of how God completely supplies all our needs. Don't you love the look of a sleepy baby at her mama's breast? She is totally satisfied physically and emotionally in her mama's arms.

> *"Yet you brought me out of the womb;*
> *you made me trust in you, even at my mother's breast."*
>
> Psalm 22:9 NIV

Describe the attributes that come to mind when you picture a nursing baby?

For a variety of reasons, I didn't get to fully experience this type of breastfeeding relationship with my own mother. It wasn't until my early twenties that I became aware of this gap in my development. I was spending time with a friend and her toddler son. Whenever he needed, he would come and snuggle on his mama's lap and nurse. She never denied him. She was always near, always available.

I was surprised by the emotions that stirred within me. I was an adult woman and yet, I was jealous of this child, fully satisfied in every way with the care of his mother. I was craving to be nurtured like this in the deep places of my soul and spirit.

However, it wasn't only the lack of breastfeeding that cultivated this void. There were other childhood experiences along the way that reinforced the lies I had received from an early age.

"(El Shaddai) is a picture of God Himself as a nursing mother- One who longs to comfort us, protect us, nurture us and gather us in His arms. He is the God who is all-nourishing and all-sufficient. El Shaddai is the God Who is Enough. He is able to totally satisfy all our needs" (Campbell 5).

Each of us needs to know and meet El Shaddai intimately. You may have been blessed with encountering His nourishing presence throughout your childhood. Or, there may have been experiences that have caused you to question and doubt His comforting, all-sufficiency in your life.

ASK HOLY SPIRIT

"Are there any lies I believe that are preventing me from receiving your comfort, protection and nurture?"

....

....

....

Break any agreements you've made with each lie.

Pray

"In the name of Jesus, I renounce the lie that *(name the lie).* I break any partnership I've formed with this lie through my thoughts, attitudes, words or actions, known or unknown. I break the power of the lie and cancel its assignment against me."

Laugh at these lies (Psalm 2:2-4)**.**

Ask Holy Spirit

"Is there anyone I need to forgive for teaching me this lie?"

Pray

"I forgive *(name the person)* for *(name the offense).* I release *(name the person)* to You, Jesus. I ask that you bless *(name the person).* Jesus, please forgive me for believing the lie. Take the lie away and everything that came with it."

WITH THE LIE & UNFORGIVENESS OUT OF THE WAY, ASK HOLY SPIRIT

"Please reveal to me the truth about who You are and how you love me."

Speak to your spirit man and plant the truth He's revealed.

Declare

"I speak to my spirit that God is *(name the truths)* and that I am *(name the truth of who you are as a result of who He is).* Thank you Jesus!"

Picture yourself climbing up onto El Shaddai's lap. Lay your head on His chest. Tell Him what you need. In this intimate place, take a still and quiet moment to receive His provision of everything you need. You are His beloved.

What deep needs do you want El Shaddai to meet this week?

When you begin to deny the reality of these needs or attempt to get them met on your own, climb back onto El Shaddai's lap. *Remember*: He is the God Who is Enough.

"I came that they may have and enjoy life, and have it in abundance (to the full, till it overflows)."

John 10:10 AMP

Jesus came so our life would overflow with His abundance. El-Shaddai is the God of abundance. Not only is He enough, He is more than enough! You were created to have all your needs met in His presence just like a nursing baby does in the presence of her mama!

day four

FAITH IN ACTION

As we satisfy and nourish ourselves on the care and presence of El Shaddai, we are better able to introduce Him to our children. We have the privilege of reflecting the mother heart of God to them in very tangible ways.

Read 2 Kings 4:1-7 & Matthew 14:14-20.

The God Who is Enough loves to multiply what we offer Him. Regardless of the size of our offering, He will take it and use it to provide for one family's daily needs or even to feed a multitude.

We are called to feed our children physically, spiritually and emotionally. But we must always feed ourselves first. On Day Three, we were practicing the habit of feasting on El Shaddai.

Like in Psalm 23:5, there may be enemies or lies circling around the table, distracting you from partaking of Him. Focus on the feast, the Lord Jesus Himself and what He is doing. The lurking enemies will fade in the majesty and intimacy of His presence. Your cup, filled with His presence and all-sufficiency, will overflow onto your children and all those with whom you come into contact.

Even when the daily offering of your mothering may feel like a measly five loaves and two fish in the face of a crowd of five thousand, it is enough. This is because God takes our best efforts and multiplies them. He stretches the results far beyond our own capacity. It's another place where He supernaturally partners with us.

To remind myself of this principle, I will often pray the reality of El Shaddai over my children as I hug them. Little ones will come close for a cuddle. I'm usually in the midst of doing something from homeschooling to cooking. I always try to intentionally stop and respond to their need for affection. However, I know their needs run deep and in a big family, they can easily be lost in the shuffle.

As I briefly hug or hold them, I ask Jesus for more. I pray He fills this child's own cup with the same loving provision He uses to fill mine. As I impart this abundance into my children, I pray and believe God is filling each vessel to overflowing.

Invite Jesus to touch and fill each of your precious vessels this week. As you interact with them and embrace them, pray and believe for the multiplication of your efforts in their lives.

Pray

"I bless you *(insert child's name)* with more of El Shaddai in your spirit and your life. May your cup overflow with His presence today in Jesus' name. May you be satisfied with His love. Amen."

Record when you intentionally imparted the reality of El Shaddai into each of your children.

Initiate a time of soaking.

Our children encounter God through us and how we mother them every day. But they also need to meet Him personally, face-to-face. Soaking prepares the way for them to encounter the tangible presence of Jesus. During this time as we wait on God, He initiates the interaction, revealing truths and taking us on adventures with Him. The goal is to set the stage and make a way for our children to have these encounters.

The purpose of designating a time to soak is to experience God's presence. Often, we feel Him, hear Him and/or see Him. After our family soaks, we always share our experience with one another. However, there are times when only a few children want to share. I encourage sharing each time because I believe God wants to speak to my children and even to our family corporately through them. Also, I want to instill in my children the expectation of hearing from God.

This takes some practice. At the beginning of our soaking journey, our kids would jump on the couch, talk and struggle to quiet themselves in His presence. Occasionally, the time would end with someone being sent to his room. Not exactly the kind of experience we were hoping for!

Don't get discouraged. It's worth fighting for this time! Keep at it. Once they really taste His presence, they'll eagerly come back for more.

Practical advice for soaking with children.

- To help prepare our hearts to soak, we sometimes sing a song like, *Be Still and Know That I Am God* using sign-language motions. I remind my children that we are quieting our hearts so we can hear God better. Encourage them to close their eyes. Having their own pillow or blanket helps define their space, limiting distractions.

- Play some instrumental or worship music. My little ones like to cuddle with me during this time. Make it cozy! Soaking is a great opportunity to enjoy His presence together.

- Typically, we soak for one to two songs but it will depend on the age of your children. When you first start practicing soaking, do so for a few minutes and build from there. Often, when the peace of the Lord comes, it is easy to extend the time. Be flexible. Follow Holy Spirit. Most of all, enjoy!

- After we soak, I provide paper and crayons and have the children draw what they saw, heard or experienced. Then, we'll go around the room and each of us (including me) will share our drawing. Or, I'll have them share verbally and I will record what was shared in a journal. It is so fun to go back and realize how God was speaking prophetically through our children and building relationship with them.

Try soaking with your children. After you finish, ask them to share what Jesus spoke to them or to draw what they saw.

Record what Jesus showed you and your children or spoke to you while soaking.

WEEK EIGHT

STONES OF REMEMBRANCE JOURNAL

How is God multiplying and bringing increase into your world? He is everything you need!

Record where He's meeting you with more than enough.

Pray

"Jesus, give me eyes to see and ears to hear the loving provision of Your presence during my day. Help me to trust that You are and have everything I need. I want to experience Your abundance!"

WEEK EIGHT

WEEK NINE

A Wise Mother Builds Her House

"Every wise woman builds her house,
but a foolish one tears it down with her own hands."

Proverbs 14:1 HCSB

day one

My husband came home one day with a little black box. I know what you're thinking: *a diamond ring or a pearl necklace*. Wrong. It was a lightweight power drill. Now, some women would be thrilled. But my use of tools did not extend beyond hammering a nail or using a screwdriver to change out batteries.

My husband intended to take me to the next level. He plugged this intimidating piece of equipment into the wall. Its red light beamed at me, reminding me that knowledge is power. Once I knew how to use it, there was no turning back. I'd be fully equipped to tackle a number of projects. Oh boy. I wasn't a very willing student.

Eric patiently gave me a short lesson about bits and screws and other stuff I no longer remember. However, I did manage to hang some curtain rods up with it. It took me a few tries but they held. That was the first and last time the drill has come out of the box. It was a thoughtful gift given with good intentions. Yet I just couldn't get past the complexity of all those pieces. To this day, I remain bound to the hammer and screwdriver.

Although my aversion of power tools has limited my D.I.Y. projects around the house, God still calls me to build. God summons mothers to partner with Him in building up their homes, their children and their husbands. He has put specially crafted tools in my hands to use with the particular makeup of my family of nine.

I have chosen to believe the gifts and strengths He has placed within me are ideal for my family's needs. For example, I love to multi-task and I accomplish the most when I have a lot on my plate. With a family of nine, there are always things to be done! I love to organize, which helps me build systems into the routine of our home so it can function more smoothly.

In addition, the Scriptures reveal other supernatural tools for building up my home and family. Obedience to implementing God's Word is the way to put these tools into practice. For example, we don't allow name calling (which doesn't mean it doesn't happen). But, we emphasize our children speaking words of encouragement as life-giving blessings over their siblings (Proverbs 18:21). During one homeschooling year, we began each day with 15-30 minutes of praise and worship. At the time, we were praying for financial breakthrough, praise and thanksgiving kept me especially focused on all that God would do and was already accomplishing on our behalf (I Thessalonians 5:18).

We have also sought to obey God's command in our thought life (Philippians 4:8). Long ago, my husband and I made a commitment to not watch R-rated movies. Our children have limited movie time and we are selective about even the literature and comic books that enter our home. We haven't always done this perfectly, but it is a standard God has impressed upon our hearts. Embracing my gifts and strengths, as well as seeking to follow God's Word, help me build a strong home with Jesus!

Every day we make choices to either build up or tear down our home by what we think, say, and do. Those Jesus calls, He also equips. He will supernaturally empower you with tools specially fitted for the tasks before you. Each of His tools is multi-purposed and has far-reaching impact. But they aren't too complicated to grasp. Holy Spirit is a wonderful teacher. He will fill your mothering tool belt with exactly what you need for the job. He won't just put the tools into your hands, but Holy Spirit will show you how to use them to build and bless your family!

DAILY DECLARATION

God has given me supernatural tools to build up myself, my home and my family. Daily, I think, speak and act wisely to build my house. Holy Spirit has anointed me and equipped me for the task!

IN A NUTSHELL

I am building my home using the supernatural tools God gives me.

day two

READ & REFLECT

Write an honest, heartfelt response to God's truth

"Even a sparrow finds a home, and a swallow, a nest for herself where she places her young - ***near Your altars****, Lord of Hosts, my King and my God.*
How happy are those who reside in Your house, who praise You continually.*"*

Psalm 84:3-4 HCSB

- As mothers, we build our house around God's presence with praise and thanksgiving. Our children then grow up in a glorious atmosphere of His presence. If you want a happy home, refrain from negativity and use your mouth for praise! Focus on filling your own life and your home with His praise, – a gateway into His presence (Psalm 22:3).

Can praise and thanksgiving be found in your home? How can you incorporate these more into your daily home life?

....

....

....

....

Choose one way from your list above and put it into practice this week.

"For everyone who comes to me and listens to my words (in order to heed their teaching) and does them, I will show you what he is like: He is like a man building a house, ***who dug and went down deep and laid a foundation upon the rock****; and when a flood arose, the torrent broke against that house and could not shake or move it, because* ***it was securely built and founded on a rock****. But he who merely hears and does not practice doing My words is like a man who built a house on the ground without a foundation, against which the torrent burst, and* ***immediately it collapsed and fell, and the breaking and ruin of that house was great.****"*

Luke 6:47-49 AMP

- Brick by brick, choice by choice, we build our lives either on the rock or on the sand. Our obedience to God's Word digs a deep and secure foundation on which we can establish our home and family. Apart from it, we cannot weather life's storms well without experiencing great destruction.

Where are you building your home: on the rock of obedience or on the sand of disobedience? Are you a doer of the Word, not just a hearer?

Ask Holy Spirit

"In which specific areas do I need to increase my obedience to Your words?"

"Some of you will rebuild the deserted ruins of your cities.
Then you will be known as a ***rebuilder of walls and a restorer of homes."***

Isaiah 58:12 NLT

- Although this passage speaks literally about Jerusalem, I believe we, as mothers, are also called to be rebuilders and restorers. God builds whereas Satan destroys. Many families are in ruins. We can strengthen our own while being a catalyst of restoration for others.

Are there any breaches or gaps in the protective walls of your home?

Ask Holy Spirit

"How can I strengthen and fortify these weak areas? What can I put into place to better protect and defend our family?"

day three

HEART-TO-HEART WITH HOLY SPIRIT

"And Jehovah spake unto Moses, saying, 'See, I have called by name Bezalel the son of Uri, the son of Hur, of the tribe of Judah: and I have filled him with the Spirit of God, in wisdom, and in understanding, and in knowledge, and in all manner of workmanship.'"

Exodus 31:1-3 ASV

The Spirit of God was given to the craftsmen of God's house, the tabernacle. Embroidery, the making of objects in precious metals, the carvings of wood and stone all required the anointing of Holy Spirit to fulfill the blueprint God had given His people.

Just as with the tabernacle, God has a specific design for each of our homes. Our home is to be a place inhabited by His presence. He will equip us with His Spirit to creatively and uniquely reflect His character and glory in our families and within the walls of our home.

If the tabernacle craftsmen needed Holy Spirit for all the detailed tasks before them, surely we do as well as we face our homemaking and child-rearing responsibilities. Rest assured, we can come to Him and receive wisdom, understanding, knowledge and much more!

What do you believe about yourself as a homemaker and builder of your home and family?

ASK HOLY SPIRIT

"Is what I wrote down true about me?"

- Take a moment to listen to His response.
- If it is true, ask Him, "*What else do you want me to know about myself as a homemaker and builder?"*
- If it's not true, circle the lies you identify in your statements.

Break any agreements you've made with each lie.

Pray

"In the name of Jesus, I renounce the lie that I'm *(name the lie).* I break any partnership I formed with this lie through my thoughts, attitudes, words or actions, known or unknown. I break the power of the lie and cancel its assignment against me."

Laugh at these lies (Psalm 2:2-4)**.**

Ask Holy Spirit

"Is there anyone I need to forgive for teaching me this lie?"

Pray

"I forgive *(name the person)* for *(name the offense).* I release *(name the person)* to You, Jesus. I ask that you bless *(name the person).* Jesus, please forgive me for believing the lie. Take the lie away and everything that came with it."

WITH THE LIE & UNFORGIVENESS OUT OF THE WAY, ASK HOLY SPIRIT

"What do you think about the way I am making and building my home?"

"What have you particularly equipped and gifted me with in order to fulfill your design for my home and family?"

Believe He has equipped and gifted you to be a homemaker! View your gifts as the supernatural tools He has supplied you with for the unique tasks you face.

Turn each gift you listed into a personal declaration. Speak these aloud over yourself.

Declare

"I speak to my spirit that I am (*name the gift*) so that my home can be (*name the purpose or design the gift fulfills*). Thank you Jesus!"

God wants you to experience His freedom in the way you make your home. In nature, there are at least nine different ways various species of birds build their nests. They might use soil, sticks, grass, a platform, a cavity in a tree or a burrow in a cliff to make their home. Our creative Heavenly Father takes pleasure in variety. He has gifted each species of bird with the instincts to build the nest that best suits their little brood in their particular habitat.

Ask Holy Spirit

"What is your unique blueprint for my home? How do you want it to function?"

Don't try to build your nest using someone else's tools or materials. Run with the vision God has given you for your home and family! I encourage you to share the blueprint Holy Spirit gave you with your husband. Together, seek the Lord for ways to practically implement it on a daily basis.

How will you implement God's blueprint for your home? Outline your plan of action below:

day four

FAITH IN ACTION

He has called you to build up your home. He provides supernatural tools given to you by Holy Spirit for this purpose. Not only do you need to receive their impartation, but these tools need to be intentionally put into practice as well.

Today we are going to discover some of the supernatural tools with which He wants to empower you!

"A house is built by wisdom, and it is established by understanding;
by knowledge the rooms are filled with every precious and beautiful treasure."

Proverbs 24:3-4 HCSB

Now receive a fresh impartation!

Read Ephesians 1:17-19.

Declare

"Daily, I grow in my understanding, knowledge and experience of who you've called me to be and what you've called me to do."

A godly home is built with obedience, wisdom, understanding, knowledge, praise, thanksgiving and encouragement. These aren't the only tools God uses to develop and strengthen our homes, but the Scripture clearly lays these power tools before us.

Read each Scripture below.

Ask Holy Spirit

"How can I specifically implement this tool to build my home?"

In my supernatural mothering tool belt, I carry...

SUPERNATURAL TOOL: *Obedience*

Scripture: *James 1:22-25*

SUPERNATURAL TOOL: *Wisdom*

Scripture: *Psalm 111:10*

SUPERNATURAL TOOL: *Understanding*

Scripture: *Psalm 119:104-105*

SUPERNATURAL TOOL: *Knowledge*

Scripture: *2 Peter 1:2*

SUPERNATURAL TOOL: *Praise*

Scripture: *Psalm 22:3*

SUPERNATURAL TOOL: *Thanksgiving*

Scripture: *Colossians 2:6-7*

SUPERNATURAL TOOL: *Encouragement*

Scripture: *1 Thessalonians 5:11*

To your supernatural mothering tool belt, add your gifts from Day Three and any additional tools God shows you. Find a Scripture that guides you in how to effectively put it into practice.

SUPERNATURAL TOOL:

Scripture:

SUPERNATURAL TOOL:

Scripture:

SUPERNATURAL TOOL:

Scripture:

day five

STONES OF REMEMBRANCE JOURNAL

Expect God to reveal surprising methods for the strengthening of your home and family. He is with you every step of the way, sharpening your tools and teaching you new ways to use them!

Keep an ongoing record of the supernatural tools He places in your hands and how to use them effectively.

Pray

"Jesus give me eyes to see and ears to hear Your vision for my home. Show me each custom tool, specifically designed for me. Bless the work of my hands as I partner with you."

WEEK TEN

Releasing the Kindgom in Your Home

"…behold, the Kindgom of God is within you."

Luke 17:21 KJV

day one

The stomach flu had hit our household. The twins were just a year old and I had unknowingly fed them blueberries for breakfast. Need I say more!

In a 24-hour period, the flu spread like wild fire through our home. We may have hit a world record with me cleaning up 20 episodes of vomiting. Yuck! It started with just one child. He had caught the stomach bug, and being highly contagious, he couldn't help but pass it along. It was just a by-product of being infected.

It is like that when we are filled with the Kindgom of God (pardon the analogy). It is inevitable our lives will overflow with His Kindgom. Our love for Jesus and obedience to His ways are contagious. We can infect others with the power of the Kindgom by simply living out our true identity as daughters of the King.

"The Kindgom of God is…righteousness, peace and joy in the Holy Spirit."

Romans 14:17 NIV

No one watches us more than our children. They are with us in our ups and downs. They observe how we handle things. They need to encounter God's Kindgom! How exciting our children can daily encounter it through our Christ-filled mothering.

The Kindgom of God is within us. We can release it to our children, our home and our world today.

DAILY DECLARATION

I am a carrier of the victorious supernatural life. The way I live is infectious. I daily bring God encounters to my children, husband, neighborhood, church and nation.

IN A NUTSHELL

As I mother my children, they experience the Kindgom of God – righteousness, peace and joy, pouring out of me!

day two

READ & REFLECT

Write an honest, heart felt response to God's truth.

"But you will receive power when the Holy Spirit comes on you;
and ***you will be my witnesses*** *in Jerusalem,*
and in all Judea and Samaria, and to the ends of the earth."

Acts 1:8 NIV

- Even though we may be called to the nations, our own family is the primary place we need to regularly testify about Jesus through our words and actions. We can make world-wide impact through our children as well!

How can you specifically share the Kindgom of God with your family today?

"If anyone is thirsty, he must come to Me and drink!
The one who believes in Me, as the Scripture has said,
will have ***streams of living water flow from deep within him.****"*

John 8:37-38 HCSB

- This is a promise! Let Him satisfy and overflow your soul. Believe in Him. He wants to let His Kindgom bubble up in you and flow out of you.

Are you thirsty? Come to Jesus. Write a prayer asking Him for the streams of living water you need to refresh yourself and your family.

"But thanks be to God, who always ***puts us on display in Christ***
and through us *spreads the knowledge of Him in every place."*

2 Corinthians 2:14 HCSB

- As moms, God delights to put us on display as a testimony of His Kindgom to our family and the world!

How and where does Jesus like to show you off? Is there anything holding you back from letting Him do so?

.....

.....

.....

.....

.....

day three

HEART-TO-HEART WITH HOLY SPIRIT

"Maybe this is just my lot in life." With the continual onslaught of financial difficulties, one day, I found myself repeating this lie. There just didn't seem to be a visible way out. I felt stuck in a cycle of poverty. I was feeling hopeless. Without the strength to fight anymore, I considered submitting to the lie that poverty and lack just may be my destiny.

Thankfully, at the time, I was also reading *Help, God! I'm Broke: Leave lack behind and step into miraculous provision* by Patricia King. The truth of His Word and the miraculous testimonies written in this book were like a lifeline thrown to me just in the nick of time.

To counter the lie trying to wriggle its way into the bedrock of my beliefs, I began declaring and releasing the promises of abundance spoken in Malachi 3:10-12. My husband even wrote them on a notecard and taped it to the dashboard of his car. Obedience to implementing God's Word is the way to put these tools into practice. When we'd face a discouraging situation and poverty would want to prove its dominating presence, we'd confess these Scriptures. Abundance, not lack, is a hallmark of God's Kingdom.

I sowed these promises and watered them with my belief. Currently, we are on the verge of real financial breakthrough. It was a long season, during which I almost gave over authority to the stronghold of the spirit of poverty. But instead, by releasing God's Kingdom promises of abundance, I held onto hope. Jesus has been our rescuer at all times!

ASK HOLY SPIRIT

"Is there anything hindering me from experiencing the Kindgom of God within me?" (It could be a belief or an incident that comes to mind.)

If there is sin blocking the way, ask forgiveness for any disobedience

Pray

"Please forgive me for (*name the sin*). Wash me with Your blood. I turn away from this sin and recommit to making godly choices. In the place of (*name the sin*), I receive (*name what He gives you*)."

If there is a lie, break any agreements you've made with each lie by praying.

Pray

"In the name of Jesus, I renounce the lie *(name the hindrance)*. I break any partnership I formed with this lie through my thoughts, attitudes, words or actions, known or unknown. I break the power of the lie and cancel its assignment against me."

Laugh at these lies (Psalm 2:2-4)**.**

Ask Holy Spirit

"Is there anyone I need to forgive for teaching me this lie?"

Pray

"I forgive *(name the person)* for *(name the offense)*. I release *(name the person)* to You, Jesus. I ask that you bless *(name the person)*. Jesus, please forgive me for believing the lie. Take the lie away and everything that came with it."

WITH THE LIE & UNFORGIVENESS OUT OF THE WAY, ASK HOLY SPIRIT

"Please show me the truth about the Kindgom of God within me."

....

....

....

....

....

....

Speak to your spirit man and plant the truth He's revealed.

Declare

"I speak to my spirit that I am *(name the truths of who you are in relation to the Kindgom of God).* Thank you Jesus!"

day four

FAITH IN ACTION

Tangibly release the Kindgom you carry over your family and in your home.

Quietly speak the Kindgom over your children while you hold your crying toddler, while your teenagers are sleeping, or as you help mediate an argument between siblings.

Whatever you need, you have access to it because Jesus Christ is living large within you in all of His fullness! **Use the following statements as declarations:**

- Where there is strife, I release peace.
- Where there is poverty, I release abundance.
- Where there is frustration, I release clarity.
- Where there is despair, I release hope.
- Where there is worry, I release faith.

Where the enemy is trying to infiltrate with evil, sow good seeds of faith, declaring His promises and releasing the Kindgom you carry within you.

ASK HOLY SPIRIT

"What other declarations of the Kingdom of God do I need to release over my family this week?"

day five

STONES OF REMEMBRANCE JOURNAL

Record the new qualities of the Kindgom you see being birthed in your own life, the lives of your children and in your home.

Pray

"Jesus give me eyes to see and ears to hear the Kingdom of God within me and around me. Thank you for making me a carrier of Your Kingdom. I want to acknowledge Your reign over every area of my life."

WEEK ELEVEN

The Joyful Mother

"... The joy of the Lord is your strength."

Nehemiah 8:10 NASB

day one

Do you ever wake up feeling like you don't have it in you to mother? But, unlike a regular nine-to-five job, you can't just call in sick and take the day off. I face this from time to time too. I wonder, "How do I rise to the occasion and conjure up enough patience for a whiny two year old, enough stamina to tackle laundry and housework, and enough vision not to get bogged down and irritated by all the little upsets of the day but to rise above them?"

As worry about these "monumental" mothering tasks passes through my head, God gently takes my hand and reminds me to change my focus. Back when my twins were newborns, God gave me a key to unlocking the meaning of Nehemiah 8:10, which I didn't understand very well.

My first response: *When I am tired and overwhelmed, how am I supposed to conjure up joy?* Then, a light went on and God showed me that I can start by enjoying! If I am focused on all the things not going smoothly, I get grumpy! But if I take a moment to laugh at my son Samuel's silly dance or smile with Joseph at the breakfast table, I begin to see my children and my mothering through God's eyes. I see my children as gifts to me. They were given to me to ENJOY! When I go through the day enjoying my children, I have strength for the tougher moments that arise.

On those days I am struggling even to enjoy, I begin with thankfulness. When my heart starts remembering and meditating on His abundant goodness in the little and big things in my life, it's hard to stay in a funk. My heart is uplifted and it is easier to enjoy! Start by enjoying your children and being thankful for them and your role as a mother. His supernatural strength will follow.

DAILY DECLARATION

I am finding joy in the Lord's presence and in His good gifts to me. Therefore, I have strength today to care for my children and perform all the tasks before me. I receive God's joy and stir it up with intentional laughter and thankfulness. As a result, my physical body and spirit are fortified with supernatural stamina and energy.

IN A NUTSHELL

I am a joyful mother because I'm anointed with the oil of joy, which results in strength!

day two

READ & REFLECT

Write an honest, heart felt response to God's truth.

"She is clothed with strength and dignity,
and ***she laughs without fear of the future.****"*

Proverbs 31:25 NLT

- Because our future is secure in Jesus, we can laugh at what comes our way! We have no fear of the future, only joy, as we embrace everything in the light of His presence.

"(She) will not fear bad news;
(her) heart is confident, trusting in the Lord."

Psalm 112:7 HCSB

What worries about your future are squelching your joy?

Now laugh at them! They are piddly in the face of the great plans the Lord has for you.

Read Jeremiah 29:11-14.

What specific plans does He have for you? Write each particular plan from these verses next to each worry you listed above. Declare His plans over those areas of worry in your life today in Jesus' name!

*"To give them…**the oil of joy instead of mourning**…"*

Isaiah 61:3 AMP

- God wants to exchange our sorrow and grief for His joy. Disappointment, loss and regret may be hanging over us. These are true feelings and experiences. We need to face the truth of these, but not wallow in them. God's ultimate plan is to replace them with His joy.

Are you ready to let them go to Him? *If not*, ask Holy Spirit to show you what is holding you back. Ask Him to prepare you to make the exchange.

Are there any areas of sadness or grief in your life?

Pray

"Jesus, I give You *(name the disappointment, loss, regret, or sadness).* Today, I receive Your joy in its place!"

"Weeping may last for the night, but joy comes with the morning."

Psalm 30:5 NLT

Receive a fresh anointing of joy! Sit in His presence with open hands. Trust Him to pour it out on you even if you don't feel it right away. He wants to overflow your cup. Let Him tickle you! Let Him make your heart dance! Rejoice in His gift of joy that overrides pain and sorrow.

"May the God of hope ***fill you with all joy and peace as you believe in Him*** *so that you may overflow with hope by the power of the Holy Spirit."*

Romans 15:13 HCSB

- Belief and trust in God are keys to being filled with all joy. The *Matthew Henry Concise Bible Commentary* says, "Discontentment and distrust proceed from unbelief." Unbelief and distrust in God will rob you of joy.

In what areas are you struggling to trust God?

....

....

....

....

....

....

Repent of any unbelief. Cross out the distrust you listed above and write the truth of who God is next to it. Start believing Him and welcome the joy that follows!

Pray

"Jesus, please forgive me for not trusting you with *(name the area).* Today, I choose to believe You are *(name the truth about God)."*

day three

HEART-TO-HEART WITH HOLY SPIRIT

She was already ten centimeters dilated waiting for the doctor to enter the room to assist her in delivering her second baby. It was the nurse who came to check on her instead. The baby was so close to arriving, she told Rose, "You could just laugh that baby out!"

A few years later, we sat in Rose's car on a chilly December evening discussing the upcoming birth of my seventh baby. I was anxious about the delivery. Rose told me how her nurse had responded and prayed this type of delivery for me.

When we think of labor and delivery, laughter isn't an emotion we typically associate with that side of birth. But Rose's baby was on her way, closer than she could have imagined. Partnering with joy, the baby would be birthed in a few exuberant pushes. A typically arduous delivery was to be made easier with the oil of joy!

Joy is an underutilized form of warfare. Laughter can bring forth breakthrough, helping us ease our way to the other side of difficult circumstances. It is such a powerful weapon. Satan uses many tactics like unbelief, distrust, sorrow, grief, disappointment, loss, regret, discouragement and fear to disables the well-spring of joy in our life. If Satan can rob us of joy, he robs us of strength. They go hand in hand.

Do you need a breakthrough? Joy can sustain you on the journey, giving you strength to endure and the grace to cross over to the other side! Let joy be the lubricant, making the way easy and the rough places smooth (Isaiah 45:2).

"Happy is the people whose strength is in You, whose hearts are set on pilgrimage.
As they pass through the Valley of Tears, they will make it a source of spring water;
even the autumn rain will cover it with blessings.
They go from strength to strength; each appears before God in Zion."

Psalm 84:5 HCSB

In what areas of your life do you need a breakthrough into a new season?

....

....

....

Are you ready to take this pilgrimage with joy? God wants you to break through, going from strength to strength. Embrace His joy and expect His strength to manifest itself in you!

ASK HOLY SPIRIT

"Is there anything hindering Your anointing of joy in my life?"

....

....

....

....

Ask Holy Spirit

"What lie am I believing about You or my circumstances?"

....

....

....

....

....

Break any agreements you've made with each lie.

Pray

"In the name of Jesus, I renounce the lie *(name the lie).* I break any partnership I formed with this lie through my thoughts, attitudes, words or actions, known or unknown. I break the power of the lie and cancel its assignment against me."

Laugh at these lies sent on assignment to squelch your joy (Psalm 2:2-4)**.**

Ask Holy Spirit

"Is there anyone I need to forgive for teaching me this lie?"

Pray

"I forgive *(name the person)* for *(name the offense).* I release *(name the person)* to You, Jesus. I ask that you bless *(name the person).* Jesus, please forgive me for believing the lie. Take the lie away and everything that came with it."

WITH THE LIE & UNFORGIVENESS OUT OF THE WAY, ASK HOLY SPIRIT

"Please reveal the truth to me."

day four

FAITH IN ACTION

"You love justice and hate evil. Therefore God, your God, has anointed you, pouring out the oil of joy on you more than on anyone else."

Psalm 45:7 NLT

This verse speaks about the Messiah. We are hidden in Christ and as His children, we too are anointed with the oil of joy (Colossians 3:3). After all, joy is a fruit of Holy Spirit fully alive within us.

As a prophetic act, anoint yourself with oil. Do it every morning to remind yourself you are receiving His gift of joy, not earning it in any way.

Pray

"Thank you Jesus, for a fresh outpouring of Your joy in me today."

Are you remaining in joy?

This week, regularly take stock of your joy level. When difficulties and frustrations confront us, it is easy to use them to justify our lack of joy. But a key to walking through these *is* joy!

Read Matthew 25:1-13.

"The smart virgins took jars of oil to feed their lamps"

Matthew 25:4 The Message

They had a supply of oil on hand to keep their lamps burning bright. Right before the virgins went out to meet the bridegroom, they also trimmed their lamps, making them ready. Candles last longer and burn cleaner if their wicks are trimmed regularly.

As His vessels, we can freely receive His oil of joy. But we must be willing to tend and feed our lamps with His supply of oil so we can thrive every day until He comes again! God holds an endless supply of joy. But we must take responsibility for maintaining the flow of His joy in our lives.

Use the checklist below to help you intentionally cultivate a joy-filled life. We want everlasting joy to continually burn bright and clean in us! His joy is a powerful witness to our children and the world. When you are lacking joy, take a moment with Holy Spirit to check the following areas.

Am I…

- ❍ Enjoying the gift of my children?
- ❍ Laughing instead of sulking?
- ❍ Being thankful for God's goodness in the little and big things in my life?

"They will come and shout for joy on the heights of Zion; they will be radiant with joy because of the Lord's goodness…"

Jeremiah 31:12 HCSB

- ❍ Renouncing any lies squelching my joy?
- ❍ Spending time in God's presence?

"…in Your presence is abundant joy…"

Psalm 16:11 HCSB

Note: *If any of these areas are tripping you up, go back through this week's study, praying again the prayers with Holy Spirit from Day Two and Day Three. Receive His joy and keep your lamp filled and trimmed, so it can shine brightly in your home!*

day five

STONES OF REMEMBRANCE JOURNAL

Expect fresh outpourings of joy as you receive from Him and cultivate your joy-filled life! For example, did you share a deep-belly laugh with someone this week? When you felt like complaining, did you smile with gratitude instead? Did you experience ease in difficult circumstances as result of your joy?

Keep record of your encounters with joy.

Pray

"Jesus, give me eyes to see and ears to hear Your joy! I give way to joy and receive it. Open Your floodgates of joy over my life. Thank you for the gift of joy on this journey. I need it."

WEEK TWELVE

The Promised Outpouring

"For I will pour out water on the thirsty land and streams on the dry ground;
I will pour out My Spirit on your offspring and My blessing on your descendants.
They will sprout among the grass like poplars by flowing streams."

Isaiah 44:3-4 HCSB

day one

When I was eighteen, I designed a purity ring to wear on my wedding ring finger. I wanted a symbol of my recommitment to purity and of my heart set apart for the Lord. I also desperately wanted to belong to someone. Who better than Jesus?

I had felt so compelled to design and wear this ring, but was not certain of its complete significance. I randomly flipped my way through the pages of the Bible, hoping somehow I'd find the answer I was looking for. Thankfully, it found me.

"This one will say 'I am the Lord's; Another will call himself by the name of Jacob;
still another will write on his hand 'The Lord's."

Isaiah 44:5 HCSB

He had already claimed me. But the ring was a reminder I truly belonged to Him, despite my sin, despite my family history. My heart began to soar! I was engraved on His hand at the cross. Now, He was written on mine.

At our wedding, I gave the ring to my husband. As the years have progressed from the age of eighteen and beyond, I have received the verses in Isaiah 44 as a personal promise from God to my growing family as well. Although they serve as one of the most significant stones of remembrance in my own journey, the promises made aren't just for me. They are for you too.

As mothers, one of our greatest privileges is to prepare the way for the Lord in our children's lives. Like John the Baptist who was called to prepare a people to receive the coming Messiah, we also bring a daily message of salvation to our children through our words and our actions. We prepare the way for them to recognize and encounter the Messiah in a number of ways – our prayers, teaching, correction, the atmosphere of our homes, and our faith, to name a few.

This is an ongoing process and at times, we can be left wondering about the fruit of our efforts. We might even question if we are doing enough and if God's truth is really taking root in our children.

For example, on different occasions over the years, my children have each struggled with being afraid of the dark. My husband or I will often pray with them, speaking over them the truth of God's presence and power in the nighttime hours, and binding any spirit of fear.

One morning, my son Caleb (age 6) shared when he is scared of the dark, he just asks God "to shine some light over me. Jesus says it's okay and comforts me. It's like joy is falling from the sky."

This reassuring testimony, however, reminds me God is constantly initiating relationship with our children. He is capable of demonstrating His presence and faithfulness to them, apart from us! Although as mothers, we play significant roles in our children's faith in Jesus, it's not all up to us. We play a part. Jesus initiated and secured salvation for all of mankind on the cross. He has promised to pour out His Spirit on our offspring. In response to His finished work on the cross, we lay hold of His promises like those in Isaiah 44, declaring and believing them for our children.

DAILY DECLARATION

I don't fret about my children's salvation. God promises to pour out His Holy Spirit on my children. He faithfully pursues them. He captures their hearts with His love. God's blessings overtake them and will be their eternal inheritance. Their thirst is deeply satisfied with the things of God, not with worldly pleasures.

IN A NUTSHELL

God has secured my children's salvation and pours out His Spirit and blessings on them!

day two

READ & REFLECT

Write an honest, heart felt response to God's truth.

"All these blessings will come and overtake you,
because you obey the Lord your God:
You will be blessed in the city and in the country.
Your descendants will be blessed..."

Deuteronomy 28: 2-4a HCSB

- Without a doubt, God's blessings are after you and your children! *Overtake* means "to come upon unexpectedly; to take by surprise" (*American Heritage College Dictionary*) and "to catch in pursuit" (online *Etymology Dictionary*). He loves to overtake us with surprise blessings around every corner! Keep your eyes peeled this week for the goodness of God coming to you in unexpected ways! Expect the unexpected!

Where have you recently been "surprised" by His blessings?

....

....

....

....

"I give them eternal life, and they will never perish-ever! No one will snatch them
out of my hand. My Father, who has given them to Me, is greater than all.
No one is able to snatch them out of the Father's hand."

John 10:28-29 HCSB

- God keeps us and our children in eternal life. No one and nothing can remove us from His loving care.

Are either you or one of your children having a difficult time experiencing God's love? What do you believe is causing the separation?

*"And I am convinced that **nothing** can ever separate us from God's love. Neither death nor life, neither angels nor demons, neither our fears for today nor our worries about tomorrow — not even the powers of hell can separate us from God's love. No power in the sky above or the earth below — indeed nothing in all creation will ever be able to separate us from the love of God that is revealed in Christ Jesus our Lord."*

Romans 8:38-39 NLT

Since there is nothing that can ever separate us from God's love, look at your above answer and recognize any lies.

Break any agreements you've made with the lies.

Pray

"In the name of Jesus, I renounce the lie that I/my child can't access and receive Your love because *(name the reason for separation)*. I break any partnership I've formed with this lie through my thoughts, attitudes, words or actions, known or unknown. I break the power of the lie and cancel its assignment against me."

Laugh at these lies (Psalm 2:2-4)**.**

Even if there is sin making you feel estranged from God, it has no power over the blood of Jesus whose love covers a multitude of sin (I Peter 4:8). However, don't let sin remain. Deal with it through prayer and repentance.

Declare the promise of Romans 8:38-39. Add any other "fears for today or worries about tomorrow" to the Scripture as part of your personalized declaration.

"So they said, 'Believe on the Lord Jesus Christ
*and you will be saved—**you and your household.**"*

Acts 16:31 HCSB

- This verse encourages us to believe not only for ourselves but for our whole family as well. Just as we have, they too will come to salvation. Keep believing!

Have you lost hope for the salvation of a child or other family member? Write the person's name below. Renew your hope in God's promise for them by writing a declaration of this verse and praying it over their life! Thank God for saving each child in your family.

day three

HEART-TO-HEART WITH HOLY SPIRIT

When we believe God has our children marked out for salvation and the outpouring of His Spirit, we approach His throne differently. This belief changes the way we pray for them. Rather than praying from a place of fear or doubt, we pray with confidence and authority.

I'm not denying there are seasons of passionately contending for our children's walk with Jesus. But we must contend and rest from the same place of confidence in what God has already done for them.

Salvation is God's gift to us and our children. When our children are walking with the Lord, we don't boast. It is a result of grace!

"For you are saved by grace through faith, and this is not from yourselves;
it is God's gift; not from works so that no one can boast."

Ephesians 2:8-9 HCSB

Our children's salvation was His plan before the beginning of time. He paid the price for its fulfillment. Now we have the privilege of partnering with Him to help bring it to pass in the lives of our children.

In his book *The Secrets of Intercessory Prayer*, Jack Hayford points to the parable of the woman and the leaven to illustrate our part and God's part in those we love coming to salvation.

> *"The Kindgom of Heaven is like the yeast a woman used in making bread.*
> *Even though she only put a little yeast in three measures of flour,*
> *it permeated every part of the dough."*
>
> Matthew 13:33 NLT

She only added a little yeast. However, due to the chemical nature of the yeast, the Kindgom of God, what she planted in the dough infiltrated every part. The dough rose and grew beyond its normal capacity. A little "Kindgom" goes a long way!

> *"God's Kindgom is like yeast that a woman works into the dough for dozens of*
> *loaves of barley bread—and waits while the dough rises."*
>
> Matthew 13:33 The Message

Here, the woman works the yeast in deliberately and intentionally, yielding dozens of loaves. Yet, before she reaps the reward for her labors, she knows she must wait while the yeast does its part. All of this, the partnering, laboring, waiting and reward, occurs in the context of everyday life, in her kitchen nonetheless.

"The outcome…a flavorful loaf (bread is a biblical type of humanity)—does indicate the result of human action, wisely partnering with practical principles, but it also reminds us of the limits of our abilities and the need to allow both the time and the space for God's divine workings" (Hayford 46-47).

Mothers have a very important part to play in their children's salvation. However, we need God's discernment to know exactly when to step in and when to sit back, pray and wait. We want our children to have their own relationship with Jesus.

The apostle Paul exhorted the Philippians to "work out your own salvation with fear and trembling" (Philippians 2:12 ESV), and so must our children. But note how the next verse says "for it is God who works in you, both to will and to work for his good pleasure" (Philippians 2:13 ESV).

Do you realize the magnitude of this promise? God is at work in our children, willing and working out His design and outcome in their spirits just like the yeast in the dough. As they mature, they need to take responsibility for their own growth as believers. But God is always within them, guiding the process.

As mothers, we bring the Kindgom to humanity, our progeny, in very practical and tangible ways. Our motherhood gives us numerous opportunities to add a little "yeast" to the whole lump of dough.

Can you trust Him to do His part while He empowers you to do yours? Write a prayer of surrender to the Lord, entrusting each of your children's spiritual journeys to Him.

Repent of any unbelief.

Pray

"Jesus, please forgive me for not trusting you with *(name the child).* Today, I choose to believe You are faithfully and lovingly pursuing him/her. You have secured his/her salvation on the cross. I trust You to bring the good work you've begun in *(name the child)* to completion."

Ask Holy Spirit

"What part do you want me to play in my children's salvation and encounters with You?"

FAITH IN ACTION

While trusting God to do His part, we also need to be intentional about doing ours. This week, practice putting your faith in God's promises of salvation and the outpouring of His Spirit into action by partnering with Him in the following four ways.

Intercessory Prayer

Impartation

Testimony

Obedience

1. Intercessory Prayer

Commit to be an intercessor for your children this week. The same promises and prayers we've been declaring for ourselves during this study, we can declare for our children as well. As an intercessor, you stand in the gap for them from the womb and beyond.

Through intercessory prayer, we agree with God's Word and stand on it, regardless of what our circumstances may testify.

❍ **Read Acts 2:17**

Pray

"God, You are pouring out Your Spirit on (*name the child*) in these last days. As a result, I declare *(name the child)* will prophesy, dream dreams and see visions. Amen!"

❍ **Read 1 John 2:12-14**

Pray

"Because of the cross, I thank You Jesus that *(name the child)* sins are forgiven. He/She is under the blood of Jesus. As a result, I declare *(name the child)* has complete victory over the evil one. Daily, *(name the child)* is coming to know the Father more intimately. I say *(name the child)*, you are strong in the Lord, filled with God's Word. Amen!"

❍ **Read 1 Timothy 4:12**

Pray

"I declare *(name the child)* is an example to other believers. He/She is full of godly speech and godly behavior. *(Name the child)* is a model of love, faith and purity to all who know him/her. Amen!"

Write at least one additional Scripture and personalize it as a prayer. Pray it as a promise over each of your children.

2. Impartation

Impart what you possess to your children through the laying on of hands. There is a supernatural transaction that takes place when we lay hands on someone.

> *"Then Peter and John laid their hands on them, and they received the Holy Spirit."*
>
> Acts 8:17 HCSB

When I first began grasping the power of impartation, I had to ask the Lord to show me what I possessed. If I didn't know what I carried, how could I intentionally give it away?

Ask Holy Spirit

"What Kindgom qualities and gifts do I possess?"

Now that He has shown you, take hold of them by declaring these truths over yourself.

Declare

"I speak to my spirit that I have the gift of *(name what Holy Spirit showed you)."*

In the book of Acts, a lame beggar asks Peter and John for money. Peter responded, "I don't have silver or gold, but what I have, I give you: In the name of Jesus Christ the Nazerene, get up and walk!" (Acts 3:6 HCSB). We might not possess every gift. But what we do have, we can give away. Peter and John were practically penniless at that moment but they offered the beggar their rich gift of healing. The fruit of their faith and impartation was miraculous. The lame beggar stood up and went walking, leaping and praising God!

This Scripture also reminds us as mothers not to compare ourselves with someone else. We may not possess a particular gift we admire in someone else. Instead of wallowing in self-defeating comparison, we must focus on what we have been given and make sure we freely give it away!

Take the opportunity to impart your Kindgom qualities and gifts to your children. You may choose to do this at bedtime, around the meal table or while they are asleep. It doesn't have to be complex or dramatic. Just give away what you have been given.

Lay your hands on each child and pray.

"*(Insert child's name),* I impart to you my gift of *(name the quality or gift).* I bless you with it. Freely I've received it and now I freely give it to you. May it increase and multiply in your life one hundred fold!"

How were these impartation experiences received by your children? Did you see any immediate fruit that followed?

....

....

....

....

....

3. Testimony

"So each generation should set its hope anew on God,
not forgetting His glorious miracles and obeying His commands."

Psalm 78:7 NLT

One key to encouraging the future generation to set its hope on God is remembering His glorious miracles of the past and present. It's powerful to remember your own family history in the context of God's supernatural intervention.

Take time around the meal table to discuss God's hand in your family's life. Recount the times He's intervened. Together, remember answered prayers. Take this opportunity to give testimony to God's supernatural power of healings and provision even if they aren't your own. However, don't discount the everyday intersection of Heaven and earth within the walls of your home. Begin recognizing His glorious miracles from this standpoint as well.

This week, revisit what you've recorded in your *Stones of Remembrance Journal*. For more miraculous testimonies, visit **www. ibethel.org/testimonies**.

What miracles did you discuss and give testimony to as a family?

4. Obedience

There is no denying encouraging the following generation in their faith in Jesus also means we need to be authentically living it out ourselves. I pray this study has been a time of deep connection for you with Holy Spirit who is changing you from glory to glory right before your family's eyes. It is so humbling and yet so exhilarating to be a work in progress before the ones we love. They need to see the process of genuine spiritual journeys worked out. Thank you for being a willing example!

"The righteous man walks in integrity; blessed (happy, fortunate, enviable) are his children after him."

Proverbs 20:7 AMP

We need to model the integrity of our faith in Jesus. However, none of us will do this perfectly. At times, we'll need to admit when we are wrong and even ask our children's forgiveness when appropriate.

ASK HOLY SPIRIT

"Are there areas in my life where I need to increase my obedience to Your commands?"

Ask forgiveness for any disobedience.

Pray

"Please forgive me for *(name the sin)*. Wash me with Your blood. I turn away from this sin and recommit to making godly choices. In the place of *(name the sin)*, I receive *(name what He gives you)."*

Ask Holy Spirit

"What changes do I need to make in order to better reflect the fruit of Your Spirit in my life? Please give me the grace (the empowerment) to make these changes."

We must live transparently before God and our family. Our conduct speaks louder than words. View a life of obedience as a powerful testimony that will assist in reaping salvation in the lives of those you love (I Peter 3:1).

day five

STONES OF REMEMBRANCE JOURNAL

Record the God-initiated encounters with His salvation and Spirit in the lives of your children.

Pray

"Jesus, give me eyes to see and ears to hear Your faithful pursuit of my children. I trust You to increase and nurture what I sow into their lives. You are the author and perfecter of their faith."

Having Trouble Hearing God?

"You open my ears to listen."

Psalm 40:6 HCSB

Because we belong to God, we have the privilege of knowing and hearing His voice. We are His sheep. The sheep know the voice of the Good Shepherd and they follow Him (John 10:27). Hearing God is not for the exceptional few. It is part of the normal Christian life.

Although throughout the study I speak about "hearing" God, there are a number of ways God speaks. You may "hear" Him through Scripture, dreams, nature, pictures, feelings, artistic expressions and other people. When discerning His message to you, always ask God, "What does this mean?" Asking God questions will lead to increased revelation!

If you are having trouble hearing God, try implementing the following recommendations. These suggestions will assist you in discerning God's voice and connecting you with His presence. My hope is they launch you into a more intimate communion with God. However, they are just a starting point. Much has been written on the subject. See the resources at the end of this section for further study.

SIMPLY BELIEVE YOU CAN

Believing a lie is an obstacle to faith. Perhaps you believe the lie that hearing God is difficult. Or, you believe the lie that everyone else can hear God clearly but you. I believed the lie that I didn't have a good, close relationship with Jesus. Because I struggled to have intimate connections with my earthly father, I projected this experience onto my relationship with my Heavenly Father.

Years ago, at a leadership retreat, I was chatting with one of the women in my small group. Out of the blue, she looked at me with piercing eyes and said, "You have a good relationship with Jesus." I was totally taken aback by her statement. I was thinking, "She doesn't know me. I don't easily connect with Jesus like others do." I stammered nervously trying to maintain composure. All the lack and inadequacy stored up in my heart was pushing against the dam I'd built to keep it at bay.

Then I realized she was speaking a truth I'd never considered. This truth confronted the lie I had been carrying deep within me. By God's grace, I grabbed on to what she said and started to believe it. I repeated it to myself when I'd doubted my ability to experience God's presence.

Do you know what happened? Things began to shift. I seemed to connect with Papa God more easily. Beginning to really sense His presence kept me coming back for more. The lie had hindered me from pursuing Him. The truth I heard made a way for me into real communion with God.

Believe you can hear God. Keep listening. Step out in faith believing you've heard His voice. He won't mislead you. An ideal place to do this is in a *Supernatural Mothering Small Group*. It will fuel your faith when you begin to receive encouragement and positive feedback about hearing His voice from others.

RETURN TO HIS PRESENCE

This exercise is especially helpful if you feel distant from God's presence. You can reenter His presence by remembering an encounter you've already experienced with Him. This trip down memory lane triggers the emotions, healing and power you felt, bolstering your faith for more!

Ask yourself, "When was the last time I remember being really aware of God's presence? What did it feel like to have God so close to me?"

Enter back into that moment. Invite Him to be here with you now. As you begin to sense His presence again, open up dialogue with Him. Ask Him other questions. Listen. Enjoy!

(As quoted by *Love After Marriage Couple's Coaching Training*)

TOGETHER, WITH ALL THE SAINTS

Our *Supernatural Mothering Small Group* is designed to be an ideal place for you to practice hearing God's voice. Your small group leader will initiate exercises crafted to lead you into His presence where you'll hear His voice. The small group setting allows for opportunities to hear God for yourself while giving and receiving prophetic ministry. A simple definition of prophecy is hearing from Holy Spirit for another person.

For years, I would see word pictures or hear phrases while praying for someone. I rarely shared these aloud. I would sometimes pray them in a round-about way but never directly. I didn't realize God was speaking to me. He was giving me prophetic words to release over those for whom I prayed. It was only in a faith-filled, prophetic community of believers that I began stepping out and sharing these words. As I did, my ability to hear from the Lord only increased. Sometimes I took risks and was wrong. But often, what I shared did bring encouragement and hope to someone else.

Sometimes, if we can't hear God ourselves, someone else will hear from God in our place. God might just use another person's caring, tangible voice to uniquely penetrate areas in our heart where we are unable to receive.

MORE INNER HEALING

Hearing God's voice doesn't require intensive inner healing sessions. However, there may be some who continue to experience road blocks in this area. If so, I encourage you to seek out the inner healing/sozo ministry in your church or surrounding community for help.

MORE RESOURCES FOR HEARING GOD

Cunningham, Loren, and Janice Rogers. I*s That Really You, God?: Hearing the Voice of God.* Seattle, WA: YWAM Pub., 1984. Print.

Toledo, Jennifer. *Eyes That See & Ears That Hear: A Parent's Guide to Teaching Their Children How to Hear The Voice of God.* Dinuba: Jennifer Toledo, 2007. Print.

Virkler, Mark, and Patti Virkler. *How to Hear God's Voice: An Interactive Learning Experience.* Shippensburg, PA: Destiny Image, 2005. Print.

Supernatural Mothering Ministries

Supernatural Mothering is a culture where God's presence and power invade motherhood.

OUR MISSION

- Create a sustainable culture
- Reveal a mother's true identity
- Affirm a mother's value
- Experience God's presence in everyday motherhood

OUR METHODS

- Our conferences are designed to launch moms into this culture! These encounter week ends equip and empower moms so they can thrive in their mothering like God predestined them to do!

- Our media platforms, like our blog, online book study, and Facebook groups gently lead moms into refreshing encounters with the living Lord Jesus right in their own homes.

  www.SupernaturalMothering.org

  www.Tips4Mom.com

  Our Facebook online workbook study

- Our studies and additional resources give moms tangible and practical tools to continue this journey on their own or in a life-giving small group setting with other moms.

Acknowledgements

Lori Byrne. You are a model for me as a wife, mother and prophetic pastor. Thank you for believing in me and paving the way!

Olivia Shupe. Thank you for recognizing my mother's heart and for investing your passion and leadership in me.

Lorraine Box. Your talent and time have taken this study to the next level! Thank you for cheering me on! Your giftings just ooze out of you and bless everything and everyone you touch!

Teresa Slater. My writing buddy. Your inner healing advice for the study was invaluable. Thank you for breathing life on my dreams!

Rose Roth. Your constant friendship and encouragement through the study has been a source of strength. Together, I can't wait to tackle what's next!

My Albany Small Group. You dared to do a study in the making. Thank you for journeying with me. Your input and insight helped refine the study. I love each of you victorious mothers. Thank you for believing in what God has laid on my heart.

Works Cited

The American Heritage College Dictionary. Boston, Mass. [u.a.: Houghton Mifflin, 1993. Print.

Backlund, Steve, and Wendy Backlund. *Igniting Faith in 40 Days*. Redding: Igniting Hope Ministries, 2012. Print.

Blue Letter Bible. "Dictionary and Word Search for *shalom (Strong's 7965)*". Blue Letter Bible. 1996-2013. 1 Feb 2013. < http:// www.blueletterbible.org/lang/lexicon/lexicon.cfm?strongs=H7965 >

Byrne, Barry, and Lori Byrne. *Love After Marriage Tools Quick Reference*. Redding: Barry and Lori Byrne, 2009. Print.

Campbell, Nancy. *The Power of Motherhood: What the Word of God Says about Mothers*. Antioch, TN: Above Rubies, 1996. Print.

Goudge, Elizabeth. *The Little White Horse*. New York: Puffin, 2001. Print.

Hay, Amy. *Spirit of the King.* N.p.: West Bow Pr, 2012. Print.

Hayford, Jack W. *The Secrets of Intercessory Prayer: Unleashing God's Power in the Lives of Those You Love*. Grand Rapids, MI: Baker Publishing Group, 2012. Print.

King, Patricia. *Help God, I'm Broke - A Practical Guide to Leaving Lack behind and Experiencing God's Abundance*. N.p.: XP, 2010. Print.

Lehman, Karl, M.D., and Charlotte Lehman, M.Div. "Immanuel Approach." *Immanuel Approach*. N.p., 2013. Web. 31 Jan. 2013.

"Matthew Henry Concise Bible Commentary." *Mystudybible.com*. N.p., 2010-2012 Web. 30 Jan. 2013.

"Overtake." *Online Etymology Dictionary*. Douglas Harper, Historian. 30 Jan. 2013. <Dictionary.com http://dictionary.reference.com/browse/overtake>.

"Pursue." *Collins English Dictionary - Complete & Unabridged 10th Edition*. HarperCollins Publishers. 30 Jan. 2013. <Dictionary.com http://dictionary.reference.com/browse/pursue>.

"Repent". Dictionary of Words from the King James Bible. . New York, N.Y., 1999.

Toledo, Jennifer. *Eyes That See & Ears That Hear: A Parent's Guide to Teaching Their Children How to Hear The Voice of God.* Dinuba: Jennifer Toledo, 2007. Print.

"Watch Your Thoughts, They Become Your Words." *Orthodoxytoday.com*. N.p., 13 June 2009. Web. 31 Jan. 2013.

"Yoke." *Collins English Dictionary - Complete & Unabridged 10th Edition*. HarperCollins Publishers. 30 Jan. 2013. <Dictionary.com http://dictionary.reference.com/browse/yoke>.

Made in the USA
San Bernardino, CA
05 July 2017